# DENBY POTTERY
## 1809 - 1997

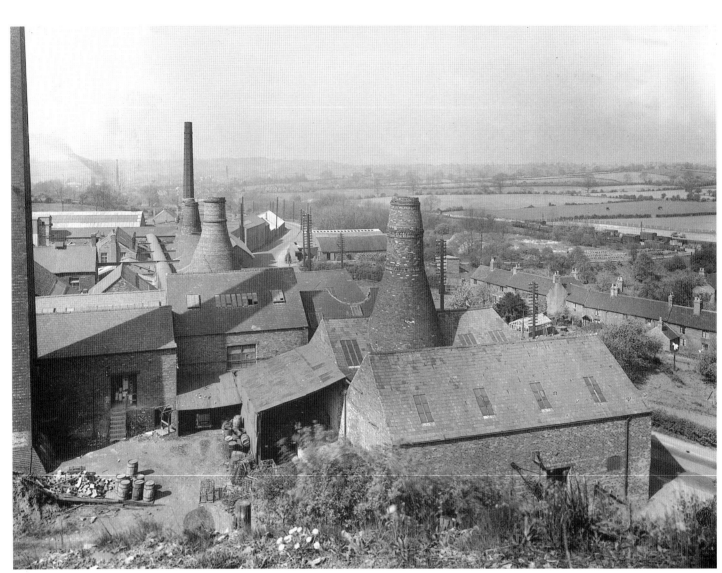

Denby Pottery in rural Derbyshire.

# DENBY POTTERY

## 1809 - 1997

## Dynasties and Designers

by
Irene and Gordon Hopwood

RICHARD DENNIS
1997

# ACKNOWLEDGEMENTS

Our interest in Denby began one dismal November day when we were confronted in our local department store by a display of stylish tableware in glowing colours. This was an original design concept, neither derivative nor overwhelmed by decoration. It did not hark back to a genteel past but succeeded in capturing the mood of the 1990s.

We searched for information on Denby in reference books only to find the same sparse facts repeated. However, by meeting Ron Brown, and reading his scholarly work on the Derbyshire Potteries and by studying *English Brown Stoneware 1670-1900* by Adrian Oswald, R.J.C. Hildyard and R.G. Hughes, we were able to contemplate the scale and complexity of Denby pottery in the nineteenth century. Our fascination with the history of the Denby Pottery was confirmed.

The authors wish to acknowledge the support, help and co-operation received from: the management and staff of the Denby Group plc, in particular, Stephen Riley and Richard Booth. To Linda Salt our sincere thanks for her invaluable help.

Former Denby managers and employees: The late Mrs. Violet Cluskey of The College, Denby, the epitome of Denby hospitality and generosity; Betty Dale, wife of the late John Dale, and her daughters, Susan and Joan; Douglas Stone, Company Chemist; Eileen White, a Company Secretary who read our original manuscript; Barbara Wood, a Company Secretary and wife of the late Norman Wood.

Designers, past and present, who discussed their work with us and explained their design philosophies: Claire Bernard, Kenneth Clark, Glyn Colledge, Richard Eaton, Gill Pemberton, the late Tibor Reich, 'Trish' Seal, Diana Woodcock-Beckering.

Museums, Libraries, Record Offices: Cheltenham Library; Denby Factory Museum; Derby City Museum, Anneke Banbury; Derbyshire Record Office, Judith Phillips and Miriam Wood; Hanley Library, Stoke-on-Trent; Keele University Library; Museum of Welsh Life; Stroud Library; Victoria and Albert Museum; Warwick City Museum, Dr. W. Allan & Catherine Roberts.

Collectors and students of Denby pottery who shared their expertise with us and generously loaned their pots to be photographed: Val Colledge, Bruce and Sue Edwards, Diana Milner, Peter Sharp, Maureen Moss, Maureen and Brian Watson, Joan and Jef Witham, Jean and Gerry of Belper, and, especially, Christine and Michael Jordan whose help with the photographic session was invaluable. We also thank Tom Powers of The Collector for his kind co-operation.

We thank Barbara Blenkinship, Len Griffin, Eileen and Rodney Hampson, Pat and Howard Watson for advice and encouragement; Lindsay and Keith Bartrop White for illustrated material; Reg and Dorothy Turner for discovering so many rare and unusual pieces of Denby pottery; Stan Hallam for background information; and Alan Peat who made available some of his personal research documents.

Our sincere thanks to Richard Dennis, Sue Evans and Wendy Wort for co-ordinating this venture.

Glyn Colledge has played a vital role, supplying unique and original information, documentation, photographs and pottery, whilst facilitating introductions to designers, craftspeople and collectors. To Glyn and his wife, Val, we offer our grateful thanks not only for this help but for their hospitality and friendship.

We hope that the Denby Group and collectors will consider that this book has done justice to the Denby Pottery and that we have established the continuing thread of Denby's design-led philosophy which links the craftspeople and artists of the nineteenth century with those of today.

I. & G.H

Photography by Mike Bruce at Gate Studios

Digital photography, print, design and reproduction by Flaydemouse, Yeovil, Somerset

Production by Wendy Wort

Published by Richard Dennis, The Old Chapel, Shepton Beauchamp, Somerset TA19 OLE, England

© 1997 Richard Dennis & Irene and Gordon Hopwood

ISBN 0 903685 52 3

All rights reserved

British Library Cataloguing-in-Publication Data. A catalogue record for this book is available from the British Library

# CONTENTS

# FOREWORD

Since I retired, the pride of working at Denby is now equalled by the fact that the company is still pursuing a good design philosophy which is keeping people in prosperous employment.

After all these years I still get a thrill to see colours in plant life, clothing, fashion and everyday things.

My philosophy has always been, 'If at first you **do** succeed, try to hide your astonishment, and if you **don't** succeed, pack it in and start again.' The rabbit, to survive, has to come out of a different bolt hole each time.

For the past three years I have enjoyed helping Irene and Gordon with their research. It brought back many happy memories for me. They were surprised at just how much I remembered and how many stories I had to tell.

It is good to see two hundred years of Denby put on the record. I feel proud that my wife, Val, and my son, Austen, will be able to read about the part that I and my family played.

Glyn Colledge
Coxbench, Nr. Derby, 1997.

Glyn Colledge decorating **Glyn Ware** c.1950.

# CHAPTER 1

# THE BOURNES OF DENBY
# 1809 - 1869

William Bourne, 1747-1823.

Joseph Bourne, 1788-1860.

If the spirit of Joseph Bourne, the founder of Denby Pottery, were to visit the current factory he would find that although the old beehive kilns had gone and the equipment had changed, the pottery was being made in a very similar way to that developed by him and his family at the turn of the nineteenth century. He would also learn that many of the descendants of the Derbyshire families whom he had employed had continued to work at the factory throughout the intervening years.

The Pottery was founded by the Bourne family and, until recently, they and their successors have either run or helped to run it. The designer Glyn Colledge, whose work exemplifies the Denby tradition, estimates that he and his ancestors served the Pottery for about two hundred and thirty years in total whilst research indicates that this may be a conservative estimate. The Sales Director until 1974, John Dale, records that no less than five generations of his family worked for Denby and three generations of the family of Norman Wood, a Managing Director, were also employed there.

Other Denby families had similar records of service – many workers who live in the adjacent village can claim that their father or grandmother or even great-grandmother worked for this remarkably stable firm.

Denby Pottery had the advantage of being the major employer in the area. At one stage, out of a village population of about 1,600, nearly a third worked at the factory. Others may have worked in local mines, ironworks, textiles, or even farming, for this is a predominantly rural area, but the Pottery was the hub of the village.

The Pottery started with the five essentials for a successful manufacturer of stoneware:
    a local bed of excellent clay;
    a nearby coalmine to fuel its kilns;
    water, supplied by a stream which ran through the centre of the site and which today exists as a small brook nearby;
    convenient communications by road, rail and canal;
    a skilled and conscientious work force.

Members of the Bourne family were potting in Stoke-on-Trent at the beginning of the eighteenth century. Records show that their first Pottery in the vicinity of Denby was at Eastwood, Nottinghamshire, just over the county border. It was owned by Richard Bourne in the mid-1700s. Richard married Rebekah (or Rebecca), the daughter of Gervase Dodd his partner at the Eastwood Pottery, and it was their son, William, born in 1747 in Eastwood, who purchased Denby Pottery.

William Bourne and his wife Edith who married in 1770, had thirteen children but, as so often happened in those days, most died in infancy. Four boys, William,

Edward, John and Joseph survived to become potters. William senior's pottery was in Belper where he produced stoneware bottles and various brownware products but potting was not his only interest. He was heavily involved in the construction of the early canals that criss-crossed the country at the end of the eighteenth century.

This was the time of the Industrial Revolution when not only canals but new roads were being opened to cater for the new industries that were developing. One such road was a turnpike between Derby and Alfreton, a few miles from Belper. The navvies digging the road came across a seam of exceptionally fine clay near the village of Denby. In 1806 the owner of the land, William Drury-Lowe, leased it to William Bourne who had realised its fine qualities. This was almost literally the foundation of the Denby Pottery. Incidentally, when the Denby Pottery opened its 'modern' showrooms in 1951, one of the guests was Lt. Col. Packe-Drury-Lowe whose ancestor had leased the land on which they stood.

At first, William senior had the clay carted to his pottery in Belper but he soon realised that it would be more economical if he had a pottery nearer to the source of his raw material, Denby. There has been a pottery at Denby since 1809 when it was merely a hut and a kiln operated by Joseph Jager (or Jagger), a former partner of William Bourne (*London Gazette* 26th January 1805). By 1812 the site had been fully taken over by William Bourne who put his son Joseph in charge.

In a deed executed in 1816, William senior was described as a 'gentleman' but his sons, William (junior), John and Joseph were shown as 'potters'. This may have been a tribute to William's wealth at the time or merely because, at the age of sixty-nine, he had retired from potting. The deed in question related to the purchase of a new Methodist Chapel at Belper, one of several that the Bournes founded. A dominant characteristic of the Bourne family was its adherence to the Methodist creed. William senior had been a devout member of the established church until he heard a Methodist preacher in Belper Market Place in 1782. He was instantly converted to the thriving new evangelical religion that was sweeping the country. From that time it was a driving force in Bourne family life and continued into later generations, not only of the Bournes but also of the Caultons, who were ancestors of Glyn Colledge on the maternal side, and the Dale family.

William Bourne's youngest son, Joseph, born in 1788, was just as devout as his father and an even more successful potter. At the time he took over the Denby Pottery the country was seething with industrial unrest. The Luddites were active in Derby and after a particularly bitter rising in 1817 three of them were hanged in Friar Gate, Derby. Fortunately for Joseph the unrest did not spread to Denby, possibly because his Methodist faith led him to treat his workers in a comparatively enlightened way.

Joseph's other brothers appear to have been less successful. William junior had been potting in Burslem,

Staffordshire, even before his father took over Belper. The Burslem factory was called Pinder, Bourne and Company and employed Robert Dale, one of John Dale's ancestors. (The Pinder in this firm's name was married to Edith Bourne.) The Burslem factory was taken over by Doultons of Lambeth when they extended their activities to Stoke-on-Trent. It is now the site of the Doulton factory in that city.

Edward Bourne was taken into partnership by his father at the Belper Pottery but he died, in 1814, at the age of thirty-one. After Edward's death the three surviving brothers combined with their father to run the Belper Pottery. William junior took little active part in the partnership and John and Joseph bought their ageing father's share and changed the name of the firm to 'J. and J. Bourne'. Joseph now had control of factories at Belper and Denby. Secure in his career, he married Alice Harvey. The couple had four sons and four daughters but only one of the sons, Joseph Harvey, survived to adulthood. The daughters, as was customary, did not take any part in the businesses.

In the year that Joseph Harvey was born, 1819, Joseph's two brothers, John and William junior died, leaving Joseph in sole charge of both factories, Belper and Denby. The Denby Pottery quickly expanded under Joseph's able management. An innovative potter, he developed improved stoneware kilns which made harder, more dense ware more cheaply than had previously been possible. He later developed a patent which improved the firing of stoneware and brownware in his kilns and was constantly seeking ways to improve and increase production.

After William Bourne senior died in 1823, Joseph continued to expand his pottery empire. In 1832 he took over a pottery at Codnor Park. It was around this time that the agitation for electoral reform was taking place, culminating in the great Reform Act of 1832. Like other liberal-minded potters, Joseph celebrated the Act with the production of several Reform Cordial Flasks, modelled to represent famous personalities associated with reform.

Shortly afterwards, in 1834, Joseph started to consolidate his group of potteries by absorbing the Belper factory and its staff into Denby. An indenture for an apprentice recruited in 1835 records that an apprentice turner would be paid three shillings a day if he produced one hundred and twenty dozen half-pint jars, less three shillings a week for his care and training. Bearing in mind that a potter's dozen could be even greater than a baker's dozen, this indenture demonstrates the sort of output demanded of workers in those days, even by enlightened employers.

When Queen Victoria came to the throne in 1837, Joseph produced a commemorative cordial flask but this was excelled two years later by a magnificent Wesley Centenary Bowl which may have demonstrated where the Bourne's main allegiance lay. Another Methodist Chapel was opened by Joseph in Street Lane in 1841, as if to extend his spiritual empire in parallel with his business empire.

A dedicated lay preacher, Joseph would not only preach in his chapel every Sunday but would prepare sermons to be read in his absence when he was on holiday in North Wales. Denby employees would be expected to attend the chapel and, no doubt, Joseph would ask them to account for any absences on the following Monday morning.

It is not known whether employees had to be Methodists but the fact is that many of the senior ones certainly were. For example, John Dale's great-grandfather Robert joined the factory from Burslem at about this time, 1842, and a Methodist history pamphlet shows that he became the chapel organist.

In the same year that he opened the chapel in Street Lane, 1841, Joseph took his son Joseph Harvey into partnership and the firm became 'Joseph Bourne and Son'. Joseph Harvey had married an efficient young woman called Sarah Elizabeth Topham who was destined to play an important part in the development of Denby. As business progressed, the Pottery expanded. Shipley Pottery

was taken over in 1845 and two years later another patent was granted, this time for an improved kiln consisting of two kilns, one above the other, with a single chimney instead of five flues. This enabled three qualities of brown stoneware to be fired simultaneously.

The excellence of the firm's work was rewarded by the presentation of a medal at the Great Exhibition of 1851. Continuing to consolidate, Denby absorbed the Shipley Pottery and staff in 1856. This was to be the last major change that Joseph would see before he died in March 1860, aged seventy-two. The following year the Codnor Park factory was amalgamated and sixty staff were acquired.

Joseph Harvey and Sarah Elizabeth had no children, unlike most of their Victorian contemporaries, so that when Joseph Harvey died on 14th April 1869, aged forty-nine, Sarah saw no alternative but to take over the firm herself.

# BOTTLES AND BEEHIVES

Beehive kilns at Denby Pottery.

From its earliest years, Denby Pottery specialised in the manufacture of salt-glazed stoneware bottles fired in rectangular kilns, and domestic ware fired in beehive kilns. Gradually utilitarian jars and containers were introduced and each item was specifically designed for the use to which it would be put. Bottles for ale and ginger beer remained in production for over one hundred years and provided the solid foundation on which the firm's future success was based.

In the nineteenth century many commodities were sold or stored in ceramic containers and because of the

durability, strength and non-porous quality of Denby's salt-glazed stoneware it was the ideal product for the time. From the earliest days Denby set the very highest standards for its ware and followed a policy of innovation and design development. For instance, in 1814 it was found that corks in some bottles were drying out too quickly and consequently deteriorating. To counteract this Denby introduced an egg-shaped bottle known as **The Hamilton**. It was designed to be stored on its side to ensure that the cork would remain moist and in good condition.

Patents were taken out in 1823 and 1847 to preserve the individuality and high quality of Denby stoneware with its special vitreous and non-absorbent features. In addition to items in the patented vitreous glazes, Denby began to use a new Bristol Glaze especially devised for stoneware, which had been introduced in the West Country in 1835. The ware produced by Denby and other Derbyshire potteries using this off-white liquid glaze was significantly greyer in appearance than that of comparable ware produced by London firms such as Doulton, in which the glaze had a pale-cream tinge.

Bottles were made to accommodate a wide variety of contents including spirits, porter, stain, ink and blacking. There was a tremendous variation in size. A small ink bottle, known as a **Penny Dud**, was sold in thousands whilst, in contrast, the skill and strength of the throwers enabled Denby to produce some gigantic storage containers. The catalogue of the Great Exhibition of 1851, held at the Crystal Palace, London, records that Denby was awarded a Medal of Distinction for a display of bottles which it presented in a large glass showcase.

Some bottles were unattributed but many had the Bourne mark, usually printed underglaze, sometimes impressed and occasionally stencilled. The 'J. Bourne Patentee' mark was introduced in 1823 and changed to 'J. Bourne and Son, Patentees', in 1841. Some bottles were marked EX which indicated that Excise Duty had been levied on the item. These were made before 1834 when the Act, as it applied to bottle manufacturers, was repealed. Some bottles which bear the Bourne Denby backstamp also include the names of the Belper and Codnor Park Potteries and this places their manufacture before 1834 and 1861 respectively, when these factories ceased to operate independently. There were many variations in the format and wording of the mark throughout the century until the introduction of the simple oval Denby mark. This mark appears most frequently on Denby bottles and indeed, the majority of marked nineteenth-century bottles found today bear the Denby stamp.

Increasingly, the name of the manufacturer of the contents of the bottle or container, or the name of the purveyor of the goods was displayed prominently as an advertising feature. Dated examples are of historical interest, especially the rare, early ones which may be found, very occasionally, bearing a trader's mark. One skilfully turned jar, in the Denby Museum, is dated 1813 and decorated with the signature of the potter, George Calton, an ancestor of Glyn Colledge, the designer, whose work for Denby in the post-World War II era is so highly regarded today.

The range of functional items was gradually extended to include insulators, spittoons, water-filters, bird fountains, plant labels and foot-warmers. Denby Pottery also satisfied a basic human need by providing kitchen wares such as bread pans, covered butter jars, baking dishes and stew pots that were long-lasting, convenient to use and good to handle.

Although the early designs of Denby Pottery were firmly rooted in the past, the progressive development of new ideas and technology enabled it to become the leading manufacturer of household stoneware in Great Britain. Its traditional, typically British ware displayed the same characteristics of strength, durability and adaptability as those in which the British people prided themselves.

## DECORATIVE WARE

Gradually more decorative pieces were successfully introduced to increase the range of products and the prestige of the firm. These pieces proclaimed the skill and dedication of the early potters, and demonstrated both the pride and compulsion felt by craftspeople to embellish and individualise their work.

**Decorative Salt-Glazed Stoneware** *was adorned with decorative sprigs outlined by a sharp tool. Rural scenes and hunting events, individual windmills, trees and flowers, the traditional toper or the head of a royal person were applied to functional salt-glazed ware from the early 1820s onwards. The range of items was extensive, varying from hunting jugs to scent bottles, from tobacco jars to puzzle jugs and from spirit and cordial flasks to commemorative ware.*

**Commemorative Ware** *in all its various forms confirmed a direct involvement with the community. Individually commissioned pieces were made but, more usually, items currently in production would be personalised and dated. For celebrating national events, a military victory, a royal accession or anniversary, a special series would be struck.*

Denby recorded for posterity not only a chronicle of the Pottery but a register of events in the locality and of special occasions in the lives of the community. Indeed Denby reflected two hundred years of British history in microcosm.

**Reform Cordial Flasks** *were a series of decorative, salt-glazed bottles which Joseph Bourne was inspired to produce by the passing of the Reform Bill of 1832. Each was moulded as the effigy of a politician or celebrity of the time, including Lord Brougham, Lord Grey, Lord Russell, Queen Victoria, Queen*

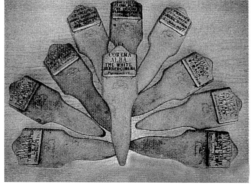

Denby plant labels originally commissioned by Professor Daubeny for Oxford University Parks in the 1850s.

Range of shapes, The Denby Catalogue, 1880.

*Adelaide, King William IV, Daniel O' Connell and John Bull. The name and a reform slogan were impressed on the front of many of the flasks. The William IV flask bore his name and the words 'Reform Cordial', whilst Lord John Russell carried a scroll in his hand inscribed with the words, 'The true spirit of Reform', and John Bull, a 'jolly man of the people' prepared to celebrate seated astride a barrel impressed with the slogan 'Success to Reform'. The flasks were impressed on the reverse side 'Denby and Codnor Park, Bournes Pottery, Derbyshire' or 'Belper and Denby, Bournes Pottery, Derbyshire'.*

The highly decorative **Wesley Centenary Bowl**, dated 1839, commemorated the hundredth anniversary of the birth of the founder of Methodism. It displayed a portrait of John Wesley and naturalistic, relief-moulded figures. It is this bowl which proclaims Denby's early commitment to the creation of decorative salt-glazed stoneware of the highest quality.

Successful home-making in mid-Victorian England demanded rooms full of furniture, artefacts and ornaments. Horizontal surfaces were used as display areas and the chimney-piece, with its accompanying mirror, shelves and cupboards, became the focal point of the room. To ensure that their pottery would take its place in this setting, Denby began to manufacture decorative items, such as specific mantlepiece ornaments and vases.

A finely sculpted bust of the Madonna modelled at Denby, was proudly shown at the Great Exhibition held at the Crystal Palace in 1851. It was acquired by Robert Dale and has been in his family ever since.

Increasingly, Denby was recognising and responding to the changing artistic climate in which art pottery was to play an important part. Admirable though the mainstream ware was, it is the celebratory and decorative pieces that fire our imagination today and which form a significant link in the chain of decorative Denby pottery which culminated a century later in the designs of Glyn Colledge.

# CHAPTER 2
# SARAH ELIZABETH BOURNE – THE MATRIARCH
# 1870 - 1899

When Sarah Elizabeth Bourne succeeded her husband she was taking charge of a substantial organisation. By that time Denby Pottery had some four hundred employees, including ninety throwers said to be using about 25 tons of clay per day. As a senior member of the local Methodist Chapel, Sarah would be familiar with many of her workers. An old Methodist booklet pictured her as the only woman amongst six elders of the chapel. As a mature, intelligent woman she was able to take Joseph Harvey's place, inspired, perhaps, by the formidable example of her Queen who had by then been on the throne for thirty-seven years. Sarah was assisted by an experienced management team including Robert Dale whose son, Christopher J. Dale, was selling the firm's products in its London saleroom.

The Pottery continued to succeed at home and abroad, winning a medal at the Sydney International Exhibition in 1879. Two years later another award was gained at the 1881 Paris Exhibition.

During this time working conditions were comparatively primitive. Much of the raw clay was prepared by men and boys trampling it with their bare feet. The working rooms were lit by candles, some of which had had to be bought by the journeymen workers themselves. The potters' wheels were turned by hand by boys who were discouraged from leaving their work at all, even for a drink of water.

Denby Pottery not only produced stoneware bottles and domestic items, but its clay was found to be suitable for industrial uses such as the production of telegraph insulators. One of Glyn Colledge's ancestors, John Caulton, invented a lathe for producing such insulators in 1883. When Robert Dale died in the following year another potential manager, George Horsley, joined the firm. He and his family were also to serve Denby for many years.

Queen Victoria's Golden Jubilee was celebrated in 1887 and commemorated by ceramic ware from the Denby kilns. The firm was becoming more involved in the production of decorative ware to diversify its output and, in 1888, commissioned a designer from London, Horace Elliot.

## HORACE ELLIOT

Although Horace Elliott's association with Denby was to continue until 1934, company records do not contain details of his work. They do, however, include a prolonged correspondence between him and Christopher Dale which reveals that Horace Elliott was as eccentric as he was talented. Inspired by the Arts and Crafts school of design, Horace combined his idiosyncratic views with ebullient, eclectic enthusiasms, ranging from Esperanto to lead-glazing.

Born on the 24th January, 1851, to Sarah Elizabeth and George Augustus Elliot, an architect, he worked as a pottery decorator and designer in London for most of his life. He created and sold his wares in Bayswater, Westminster, Chelsea and, finally, Streatham Hill. Many of his designs were registered with the Board of Trade and he regularly exhibited with the Arts and Crafts Exhibition Society.

In common with other supporters of the Arts and Crafts movement, Horace had a nostalgic vision of honest craftsmanship in an atmosphere of rural simplicity. He found such a setting in 1880 when on a business visit to Wales. After calling at a pottery run by a Mr. Doel of Doultons, he discovered the country kiln operated by the Jenkins brothers, David, John and Edwin, of Ewenny. Although none of the brothers spoke much English, a bond of craftsmanship must have been established and Horace became enchanted by this vision of a peasant pottery. For the next thirty years he visited Ewenny every year, usually staying with the Jenkins family for a few weeks. In 1908, however, he lived there for six months and, with David Jenkins, created many characteristic pieces including commemorative ware, plant pot stands and pitchers with applied decorations of natural leaves. A jug, in the form of an angel, he designed at Ewenny was later made in stoneware at Denby.

During the 1890s Horace developed an enthusiasm for sgraffito decoration which he used to great effect on his work for both Denby and Ewenny. An interest in

Sarah Elizabeth Bourne, 1823-1898.

Horace Elliott (second figure on the right) with David, John and Edwin Jenkins at the Ewenny Pottery.

Esperanto stemmed from his friendship with a Miss Turberville of Ewenny Priory. He even inscribed Esperanto mottoes on some of his pots. Others he decorated with Welsh sayings as a tribute to his colleagues in Ewenny.

Horace Elliott's registered trade mark was the fleur-de-lys. On one occasion he made fourteen tiles at Ewenny spelling out his name for his London shop front; the fleur-de-lys divided the two words. Comparatively few examples remain of Horace's work for Denby despite his long association with the factory, but his position as one of their first decorative designers is firmly established. During his long career in pottery he was associated with other Arts and Crafts artists, including the well-known C.H. Brannam of the Barnstaple Pottery.

As the nineteenth century drew to a close, Denby continued to prosper. Christopher J. Dale's son, Alex, joined him in the firm's London saleroom in 1891. Two years later, a potential managing director, Joseph Wood,

joined the firm in a very junior capacity. In the year of the Queen's Diamond Jubilee, 1897, the Dales took on a London-based traveller, E. Sanderson, who must have sold hundreds of Denby's Jubilee beakers.

In her thirty years 'reign' Sarah Elizabeth increased sales at home and abroad and extended Denby's product range to include distinctive kitchen and tableware, and some decorative items. As well as being a dynamic and successful businesswoman, Sarah continued in her chapel activities and maintained a philanthropic attitude towards her employees. She developed a savings scheme, supported by company funds, to encourage workers to set aside some of their earnings for future contingencies. At her beautiful home, Netherlea, in nearby Holbrook, to which she moved in 1884, Sarah employed many domestic servants, indoor and outdoor.

Sarah Elizabeth's career coincided with the very earliest developments of female emancipation and independence. Although male suffrage had been extended in 1867 the vote was not yet available to women. Nevertheless, the 1867 Act spurred women to seek political power. Domestically, working women were achieving freedom to a limited extent by the invention of carpet sweepers and washing machines. Meanwhile, Sarah Elizabeth Bourne was exerting real economic power – thirty years before Emmeline Pankhurst formed the Women's Social and Political Union in 1903. A sexual revolution was in the air and women generally were beginning to resent their inferior political status. It must have seemed ironic to an intelligent woman like Sarah that whilst she exerted economic power over the three hundred men she employed, they had the right to vote while she did not.

Sarah's power lay in her control of the Denby empire. In a lesser way she demonstrated her personal independence

Left to right: John Caulton and Robert Dale, 1837.

by insisting on driving her own carriage and pair. By the time she died, Sarah Elizabeth Bourne was a very rich woman. As she had no children she distributed her estate amongst her nephews. Many other relations and servants benefited as well as various good causes including Dr. Barnado's Homes and local hospitals. Incidentally, Netherlea became a Barnado's home many years after her death. Her will ensured that her nephews, Joseph Bourne-Wheeler and John Henry Topham took over the factory and included conditions that bound them to Denby for the immediate future. She died at the age of seventy-five on the 7th August 1898.

The following year John Caulton, then aged eighty-one, decided that it was time for him to retire before he too died 'in harness'. He died two years later, in the same year as Queen Victoria.

As Sarah Elizabeth had intended, her place was taken by Joseph Bourne-Wheeler, a direct descendant of the Bournes, who had worked for her since 1877, and John Topham, a nephew from her side of the family.

# GOOD HOUSEKEEPING

Products listed in advertising material of the 1870s were categorised into four groups – utility, kitchen, table and decorative ware, indicating the wide range of items in the Denby repertoire. In 1880, an advertisement in *The Pottery Gazette* focused on telegraph insulators and battery cells reminding the pottery trade of the significant contribution that Denby was also making towards the manufacture of high-quality industrial ware.

In 1885 the same magazine listed the following items for sale: stoneware bottles, fowl fountains, water filters, foot-warmers, brown-and-white glazed domestic ware, teapots, coffee jugs, plain and Toby beer jugs. Bottles and brown salt-glazed stoneware for cooking and storage remained an important part of production at Denby but the emphasis was gradually directed towards kitchen and tableware.

**British Fireproof Cookware** *which could be used on an open fire, was issued in 1887, thus adding another important category of ware to the firm's already extensive output of brown-glazed ware. It included not only stew pots, saucepans and milk boilers, but also teapots, coffee pots and jugs.*

British Fireproof ware, Denby Catalogue, 1904.

New glazes were applied to tableware and allied items which were then marketed according to their glaze. When two different colours were used on one pot they would often be separated by a simple, decorative beaded line. During the latter part of the nineteenth century some tableware was decorated with a roughened band.

**Denby Ware** *was the name given to many of the firm's products in which the upper part of a pot was glazed in brown and the lower part covered with a transparent glaze through which the natural, stone-coloured clay body could be seen. Today it is referred to as Denby Colours.*

**Chocolate Ware** *was first made in 1895 and glazed in dark-brown with a smooth upper part and contrasting textured base.*

**Brown** *and* **Green Stoneware** *was a comparatively colourful range in which the upper part of each pot was glazed in a rich brown with the lower half glazed green and divided from the upper by a neat line of beading.*

New art glazes were occasionally applied to tableware of which the peacock-green glaze of 1897 was particularly noteworthy.

Towards the end of the century Sarah Elizabeth Bourne confidently advertised an extended range of utility, kitchen and tableware and was making tentative references to decorative vases. Denby stoneware was a staple product in daily use. Its successful progress into the next century was ensured by innovation and by the constant development of popular ranges and new glaze effects.

## DECORATIVE WARE

**Salt-Glazed Figured Stoneware** *included magnificent figured hunting jugs with a capacity of up to eight pints together with teapots, beakers, mugs and loving cups. Spectacular game-pie dishes and large salad bowls exemplified the art of the potter with high-quality modelling and fine detailed embossments. It was during the 1870s that a variation on the original sprigged windmill was introduced on which a door and three arched windows were depicted.*

**Derby Terracotta** *involved a change of medium and of technique. Completely different in style from Denby's usual strong simple shapes, figured urns in the classical style were made in a wide variety of sizes, together with overall textured vases, some with prominent handles, Indian scent jars and round plaques*

Little is known of the earliest art pottery produced at Denby but it is believed to have consisted mainly of vases and flower tubes decorated with coloured glazes. Given the generic name of Danesby Ware, it was marketed as such in 1886 and this name continued to be used until the 1960s.

The name Danesby was derived from the name of the area around Denby where the Danes settled many centuries ago and which was known as Danes-by or Danes village.

**Denby Majolica** *was the name given to mottled ware, heavily glazed in dark-blue and tan, and very rarely in dark green and tan. It was made around the turn of the century, on typically Victorian shapes. Stylistically it bore no resemblance to the relief-moulded English Victorian majolica with which it was contemporary.*

Between 1870 and the early part of the twentieth century the influence of artistic developments such as the Aesthetic Movement, the Arts and Crafts Movement and the Art Nouveau Style was being reflected in the designs of British pottery. Small studios, or individual studios within large industrial potteries, were being set up by artists and designers to produce hand-crafted art pottery.

By the 1870s the art department of Doultons of Lambeth was thriving and in 1873 the Martin Brothers were setting up their first studio in Fulham, before moving to their own pottery in Southall. It may have been that these developments and the success of the art pottery

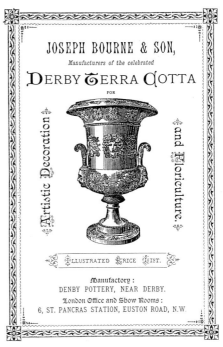

Derby Terracotta, Denby Catalogue, 1886.

being made at the neighbouring Langley factory influenced Sarah Elizabeth Bourne to commission work from Horace Elliott, a freelance designer.

## HORACE ELLIOTT

Horace Elliot is known to have designed Egyptian, Oriental and Byzantine styled vases, fern pots, plant pots, candlesticks and commemorative ware. His most significant contribution to Denby pottery lies in his blue and cream sgraffito designs.

**Sgraffito Ware** *based on the original and individualistic shapes achieved by Horace Elliott was glazed in cream and decorated in fine sgraffito-work with cross-hatching in a deep blue. Mottoes and inscriptions embellished and distinguished his work which was stamped with a diamond containing a fleur-de-lys.*

## JAMES WHEELER

Sarah Elizabeth also encouraged an artistic member of her family to apply his considerable talents towards creating a series of art pottery for Denby.

Pots marked 'J.C.W. Belper' or J.C.A.W. are believed to have been the work of James Wheeler, an amateur artist and dilettante who was the brother of Joseph Bourne-Wheeler. A selection of his drawings, almost identical to those on Denby pottery, has been preserved in a sketch book now in the possession of his descendants.

**Sgraffito Ware** *with sensitive and delicate illustrations of birds was quite different in style from the strong lines and bold decorative effects created by Horace Elliott, displaying more of an affinity with the work of Hannah Barlow at Doultons of Lambeth. Blue sgraffitoed vignettes of baby ducks, hens and cockerels were displayed under a transparent glaze.*

The artistry of the individual was now reflected and accorded recognition.

Decorative salt-glazed stoneware, Denby Catalogue, 1912.

15

Employees at the Denby Pottery, c.1900.

John Topham, joint manager, 1898-1907.

Joseph Bourne (to the right of central chimney) with members of his workforce, c.1840.

Denby Pottery employees at the Centenary celebrations, 1909.

# DECORATIVE DENBY POTTERY

**Reform Cordial Flasks**, c.1832 with the **Wesley Centenary Bowl** dated 1839. Tallest 8ins (20cms).

Salt-glazed loving cup dated 1858, 19th-century puzzle jug, two hound-handled tygs, small pot and mugs commemorating the Diamond Jubilee of Queen Victoria. Tallest 10ins (25.5cm).

'Beauty combined with utility'. The Hannah Outram butter churn dated 1835 with a selection of 19th and early 20th-century items, bottles, miniature travellers' samples, a fowl fountain, a housekeeper's jar and a vase. Tallest 12½ins (32cms).

19th-century salt-glazed jugs and mugs with central jar signed 'George Calton, 1813'; centre right is a personalised jug marked 'W. Dale Pilesley, 1839' and centre left, a jug by Horace Elliot c.1900 inscribed 'Few handicrafts can with our trade compare, We make our wares of what we potters are = clay'. Tallest 8½ins (21.5cms).

19th-century ink wells, condiment containers and bottle far right. Tallest 5½ins (13.5cms).

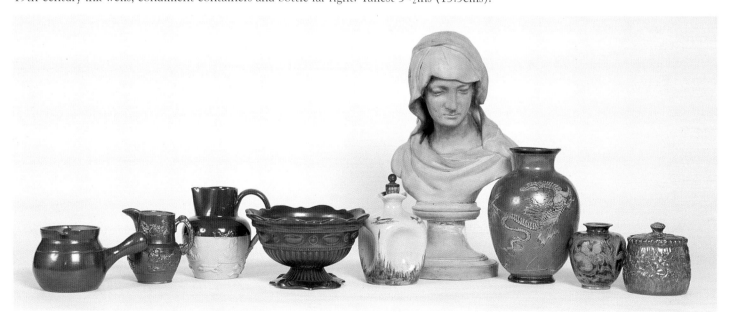

**The Dale Collection**: Madonna, modelled at Denby, c.1850; 'the first Denby pipkin'; two salt-glazed jugs; **Vulcan** ware bowl; decanter by James Wheeler; dragon vase, small vase and lidded pot each inscribed Martin Brothers and Denby, 1909'. Tallest 17ins (43cms).

**Denby Majolica**, c.1890. Tallest 13¹/₂ins (34.5cms).

**Sgraffito Ware** by Horace Elliot, c.1900 and two **Butterfly Ware** vases, c.1910. Tallest 7¹/₂ins (43cms).

**Sgraffito Ware** by James Wheeler, c.1900. Tallest 9¹/₂ins (24cm).

Terrestrial globe supported by four lions, commemorating the British Empire Exhibition, 1924, and contemporary tube-lined ware. Tallest 10$^1$/$_2$ins (26.5cms).

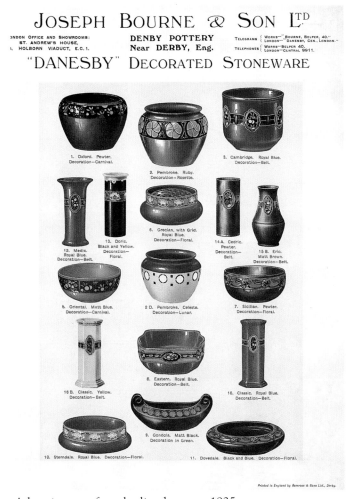

Advertisement for tube-lined ware, c.1925.

Advertisement for tube-lined ware, c.1925.

Title pages of **Danesby Advertising Catalogues,** c.1930.

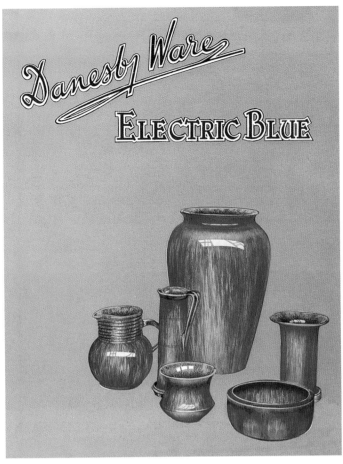

Electric Blue.

Orient Ware.

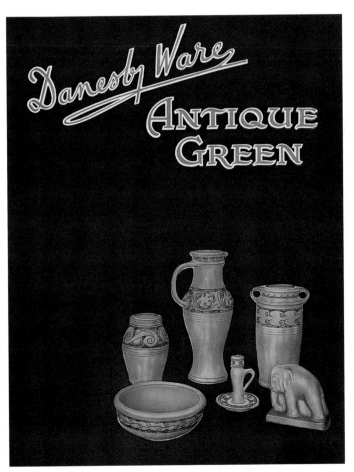

Antique Green.

All the articles illustrated on pages 34 and 35 are supplied in Meadow Green colour at the same prices as for Electric Blue under the following pattern numbers and names :—

701 Middleton
702 Brassington
703 Ilam
704 Lathkill
705 Riber
706 Alton
707 Hardwick
708 Edale
709 Ashwood
710 Wynne
711 Castleton
712 Chevin
713 Lamp
        Candlestick
714 Cressbrook
715 Willersley
716 Derwent
717 Elephant
        Book End

Meadow Green.

**Electric Blue**, c.1925. Diameter 12ins (30.5cms).

**Electric Blue**, c.1925. Tallest 9ins (23cms).

**Antique Green,** with **Silver Grey** vase far left and **Meadow Green** vases and jug, far right. c.1930. Tallest 9½ins (24cms).

**Orient Ware**, c.1926. Tallest 12¹/₂ins (32cms).

**Orient Ware**, c.1926. Tallest 12ins (30.5cms).

**Moorland**, c.1930. Tallest 8ins (20.5cms).

**Regent Pastel**, c.1933. Tallest 11ins (28cms).

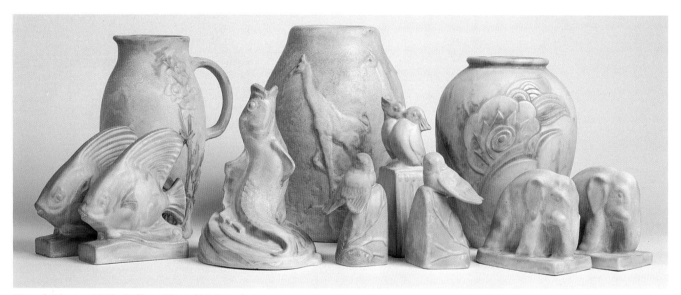

**Pastel Blue**, c.1933. Tallest 12ins (30.5cms).

**Pastel Blue** and **Regent Pastel** with **Featherstone** lamp base, vase and jug, c.1936. Tallest 12½ins (32cms).

**Tyrolean Ware** with two **Gretna** jugs and bowl; extreme left and right, **Greenland** jug and mug, c.1937.

**Tyrolean Ware** in old gold glaze, c.1937, **Garden Ware** penguin, c.1934. Tallest 17½ins (44.5cms).

**Garden Ware** with lamp base and fish tray, c.1934. 10ins (25.5cms).

**Floral Pastel**, c.1937. Tallest 13½ins (34cms).

**Herbaceous Border**, c.1935; **Folkweave** plaque and **Tibet** jug, c.1939; **Gay Border** vase, c.1948. Diameter 13$^{1}/_{2}$ins (31cms).

A proliferation of Denby rabbits in coloured glazes with one complete family in **Orient Ware**, c.1930s. Tallest, 10$^{1}/_{2}$ins (26.5cms).

**Byngo**, **Fido** and friends, c.1930s. Tallest, **Byngo**, 6$^{1}/_{2}$ins (16.5cms).

**Ivory Pastel**, c.1939. Tallest 11¹/₂ins (29cms).

Lambing time in rural Denby, c.1930s. Tallest 11ins (28cms).

Novelties including 'Wilfred the Hot Water Rabbit', the 'Skier', the 'Golfer', and 'hats off' to the Army, Navy and Air Force, c.1930s. Tallest 10³/₄ins (27.5cms).

**Antique**, **Festive** and **Tally Ho** with rare undocumented **Jacobean Ware** bowl and poodle tray by Albert Colledge, c.1948. Tallest 8ins (20.5cms).

Two early studio vases decorated by Glyn Colledge, with six **Original Glyn Ware** bowls displaying tube-lined animals, and **Glyndebourne** vases, jugs, bowl and lamp-base, c.1948. Tallest 14ins (35.5cms).

**Glyn Ware**, c.1950. Front right, early 'one-off' carved plaque; four post-Denby plaques and bowls with hand-painted birds. Diameter of plaque 15$\frac{1}{2}$ins (39.5cms).

**Glyn Ware** with **Bo-Peep** mug, c.1950 and **New Glyn Ware** tray, c.1954. Tallest 9ins (23cms).

**Glyn Ware** with hunting beakers, c.1950. Tallest 8¹/₂ins (21.5cms).

**Glyn Ware** plaques and bowls, c.1950. Diameter 12ins (30.5cms).

**Tigo Ware** with **Florence**, **Espanola** and the **Madar Bird**, c.1956. Tallest 15ins (38cms).

**Tigo** decorative tableware, c.1956. Tallest 10³/₄ins (27.5cms).

Left to right: **Hazelwood** bowl, **New Glyn Ware** bowl, **Crystalline** vase, two **Tapestry** vases and jug, **Ferndale** vase, **Celadon** jug and two bowls, **Cretonne** vase and bowl, and **Freestone** vase, mid-1950s. Tallest 11¹/₂ins (29cms).

**Cheviot** vases, c.1956. Tallest 19ins (48cms).

**Cloisonne** and **Cheviot** with **Classic** jug and small **Burlington** tray (front row, second left), mid- to late-1950s. Tallest 9ins (23cms).

**Glynbourne**, c.1960. Tallest 13ins (33cms).

Four **Egyptian** plates, **Minaret** plaque and two vases, two studio vases by David Yorath, **Flamstead** vase and small bowl, **Savannah** vase and jug with experimental decoration by Glyn Colledge, and rare organic-shaped jug, 1960s and 1970s. Tallest 12³/₄ins (32.5cms).

**Cascade**, c.1978. Tallest 13¹/₂ins (34.5cms).

**Origins**, Denby advertising photograph, c.1987. Tallest 13ins (33cms).

# CHAPTER 3

# THE CENTENARY – THE WAY AHEAD
## 1900 - 1915

The new regime of Joseph Bourne-Wheeler and John Henry Topham was now in full control at Denby.

John Topham was a ruthless manager who would smash the whole of a thrower's output if he was not satisfied with its quality. On one occasion he sacked nine kiln workers simultaneously during Belper Wakes, (an annual holiday at a nearby town), because he felt they had neglected their work. Joseph Bourne-Wheeler was reported to have been less ruthless but well-respected.

Britain was still involved in a bitter struggle with the Boers in South Africa. In 1900 the Siege of Mafeking was relieved and Denby celebrated with a commemorative beaker. More commemorative ware proclaimed the Coronation of Edward VII in 1902, but its sale must have been disrupted by a disastrous fire in the following year that destroyed Denby's London warehouse and offices, near St. Pancras Station. The resilient firm soon recovered by opening superior premises at number 23, Euston Road.

At this time all the work was produced on the potter's wheel except for the pressing of foot-warmers and similar products.

In 1904, in rural Denby, Albert Colledge, then a young man of thirteen joined the firm as a caster. A grandson of John Caulton, he started work in this comparatively humble position before his talent prevailed and he became Denby's chief designer.

The firm's range of products was extended as it increased in strength. A new salesman, J. Rushton, was appointed in 1905 to cope with increasing sales but the firm's prosperity was not sufficient to persuade John Topham to remain at Denby. He left in 1907 leaving Joseph Bourne-Wheeler at the head of the firm, a position he was to hold until 1942.

In 1908, to prepare for its centenary, the firm had an imposing new frontage built to give a more modern aspect

Invitation to the Centenary celebrations.

to the group of bottle ovens and warehouses that comprised the old Pottery. The centenary celebrations on 7th August 1909 took the form of a commemorative fête on the Denby cricket ground. Over five hundred employees and former employees attended and enjoyed sports and lavish refreshments. They were entertained by the Denby Brass Band and, after tea, heard speeches by Joseph Bourne-Wheeler, Christopher Dale and George Horsley, the General Manager. Joseph Bourne-Wheeler recounted the history of the Pottery and Christopher Dale proposed the toast, 'Success to Messrs. Joseph Bourne and Son ' (as the firm was still known).

In a progressive speech Mr. Dale remarked that this was the day of young men and 'young women too' and went on to say that young women of the day would exercise a greater influence in commercial and political matters than had women in the past. These remarks may well have been inspired by the example of the remarkable Sarah Elizabeth Bourne. George Horsley seconded the proposition with a speech praising the Bourne-Wheelers and urging those present to work harder for the continued success of the firm and, incidentally, more wages.

Commemorative medals depicting the Bourne-Wheelers on one side and an image of the factory on the other were distributed and Joseph Bourne-Wheeler was presented with a solid silver salver bearing an inscription that included the names of the potteries that had been taken over by Denby: Belper, Shipley, Codnor Park and Eastwood. The salver was presented by William Mitchell who had been with the firm for sixty-four-and-a-half years. Mrs. Bourne-Wheeler received a silver jewel box engraved with her monogram. *The Pottery Gazette* report concludes that 'the remainder of the day was spent in sports and friendly intercourse.'

Denby Centenary commemorative medal.

Members of the management who attended the centenary celebrations, 1909. From left to right: Christopher J. Dale, Joseph Bourne-Wheeler, George Horsley, E. Sanderson, Alex J. Dale and J. Rushton.

*The Pottery Gazette* reporter who visited the factory in the centenary year described how the premises had been improved and extended 'almost out of recognition'. The latest machinery and appliances had been introduced but original methods were still used that were peculiar to Denby. There were twenty-two kilns and ovens with an enormous output which was stored in a huge warehouse, 122ft. long and 42ft. wide. The reporter went on to describe the wide variety of Denby products, from christening mugs and hunting jugs to cremation urns, remarking on the firm's consistently progressive policy.

In the following year Christopher Dale again moved Denby's London showroom, this time to St. Andrew's House on the Holborn Viaduct. To increase the sales of cookware Denby introduced a handbook on the use of their casseroles in addition to the regular production of 'Bourne's List', a catalogue of all wares available. By now an international company, the firm exhibited at Turin in 1911, the year of George V's coronation, another occasion for the production of commemorative ware.

In his speech at the centenary celebrations, Christopher Dale remarked that if he lived until the spring he would have worked for the firm for fifty-three years. He did, in fact, live for a further three years.

World War I broke out in 1914 but the firm told *The Pottery Gazette* that business was assured despite the war.

# STONEWARE FOR ALL SEASONS

Denby maintained its output of bottles and containers for the brewery trade and chemists while continuing to manufacture the myriad traditional stoneware items so essential for home, trade and industry. Denby manufactured, as part of their stock-in-trade, 'giant' ginger beer bottles and handled bottles basketed in white wicker. Customers ordering a sizeable quantity were encouraged to incorporate the printing of their trade name and product in black underglaze, as a permanent advertising feature. Samples of advertising specialities such as match-strikers and ashtrays were displayed at Denby and at the London showrooms.

The severe frost and snow of the winter of 1900 ensured that the already popular hot-water bottles would be a priority purchase for the shivering British public. Originally they were salt-glazed and marketed as bed bottles, feet bottles, perambulator foot-warmers and sloping carriage feet-warmers. Miniaturised hand-warmers, sometimes with a chain carrying-handle, included the flat **Dainty Muff** and the easy to handle **Egg Muff Warmer**, so named because of its shape. A hand-sized version of the traditionally shaped hot-water bottle was also available.

Retailers were offered the opportunity to have a free advertisement placed on any significant order of steam-tight, screw-stoppered foot-warmers. These durable items remain today as reminders of the traders who sold them so many years ago. Such was the demand that Denby always kept a stock of their foot-warmers ready to receive a printed advertisement to ensure prompt delivery.

Novelty foot-warmers were an added attraction. **The Bungalow** was cream- or clear-glazed, flattened and appropriately illustrated whilst the similarly glazed **Arctic** pictured the Frozen North complete with igloo and explorer. The now rare **Motor** foot-warmer in the shape of a bag 19ins. long, glazed in brown or in green, was designed for long, cold journeys and a new mechanised life-style.

Kitchen storage jars with distinct enamelled lettering, as permanent as the containers themselves, were made with white letters on a dark ground and vice-versa.

Throughout the early part of the twentieth century, advertising catalogues show that a major part of Denby's output consisted of British Fireproof, Chocolate Ware and Brown and Green Ware.

**British Fireproof (Green)** *was an alternative colour-way issued in 1906. By 1911 it included no less than a hundred separate pieces.*

**Chef Ware**, *a new French style of cookware issued in 1909, consisted of stew pots, casseroles, marmites and saucepans glazed in brown. Pieces that were unglazed or partially glazed had a red interior. They reflected the influence of French cooking vessels and were ideal for the slow cooking of cheaper cuts of meat and vegetables and must have proved invaluable during the wartime years. Each piece was marked with the Chef Ware backstamp.*

**Fireproof Cooking Earthenware** *was an inexpensive version produced three years later using French imported clay.*

JOSEPH BOURNE & SON, DENBY POTTERY, NEAR DERBY.

## GINGER BEER BOTTLES.

JOSEPH BOURNE & SON's Ginger Beer Bottles have the reputation of a century for their non-absorbent quality, strength, and durability. They are made in every known variety of glaze, and can be supplied with mouths plain for Corks or tapped for Screw Stoppers.

**The Old Brown Salt Glazed Bottle** is supplied in very large quantities, being particularly popular in London and suburbs. The name and address is impressed into the bottle, either on shoulder or side. Trade Mark can be added if desired.

**The White Glazed Bottle with Buff Top** is also very largely used, the printing of the name in black under glaze being a leading feature. This forms a neat and attractive label, as well as a useful and permanent advertisement. These bottles may also be had in several other varieties of colour; all white, all buff, rich brown glaze, and white with blue or green top, &c.

**Ginger Beer Bottles, Champagne Shape,** are manufactured in the same materials and colours as quoted above.

They can be supplied either with Cork mouths or tapped for Screw Stoppers, also fitted with the Porcelain Swing Stopper which has recently become popular.

*Samples and Prices of Ginger Beer Bottles may be had on application.*

### SCREW STOPPERS FOR GINGER BEER BOTTLES.

These are made in Stoneware, and are of the standard thread. Name and address of customer can be printed in black on head.
Price 5/6 per gross.
Vulcanite Stoppers, 6/- per gross, or Lignum Vitae Stoppers 5/6 per gross.

Ginger beer bottles, Denby Catalogue, 1909.

---

JOSEPH BOURNE & SON, DENBY POTTERY, NEAR DERBY.

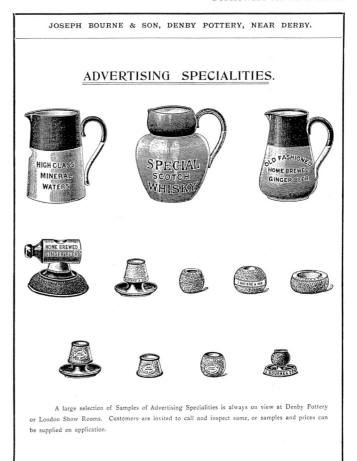

A large selection of Samples of Advertising Specialities is always on view at Denby Pottery or London Show Rooms. Customers are invited to call and inspect same, or samples and prices can be supplied on application.

Advertising specialities, Denby Catalogue, 1909.

---

JOSEPH BOURNE & SON, DENBY POTTERY, NEAR DERBY.

## HANDLED BOTTLES.
### (WHITE AND BUFF.)

| | qt. | 3 pt. | 2 qt. | 3 qt. | 4 qt. | 6 qt. | 8 qt. | 12 qt. | 16 qt. | |
|---|---|---|---|---|---|---|---|---|---|---|
| Plain Mouth ... ... | 4/- | 5/6 | 6/9 | 7/6 | 10/- | 13/6 | 18/- | 30/- | 40/- | per doz. |
| Mouth for ordinary Vulcanite Stopper } | 4/6 | 6/- | 7/3 | 8/- | 10/6 | 14/6 | 19/- | 32/- | 42/- | ,, |
| With Stoneware Screw Stopper } ... | 7/- | 8/6 | 9/9 | 10/6 | 13/6 | 17/6 | 22/- | 35/- | 46/- | ,, |

Extra for Tap Holes, up to and including 4 qt., 2/-; above 3/- per dozen.
Name and address impressed without extra charge.

Name or Trade Mark printed on shoulder, under glaze, 6d. per dozen extra up to and including 4 qt.; 1/- per dozen above. Large printed design on side, 2/- per dozen extra. A small charge for stamp will be made with first order.

### GIANT BOTTLES FOR BREWED GINGER BEER.
#### (IN WHITE AND BUFF STONEWARE.)

With Stoneware Screw Stopper and tap hole, with name or trade mark printed under glaze.

Stamp for printing charged extra with first order.

| 1 gal. | 2 gal. | 3 gal. | 4 gal. | 4½ gal. |
|---|---|---|---|---|
| 18/6 | 27/6 | 40/6 | 51/6 | 56/6 |

per dozen.

Best Boxwood Taps, 2/6 per dozen.
Cork Collars to fit, 1/- per dozen.
Hughes' Patent Wire Handles, 2/6 to 3/6 per dozen, according to size.

### HANDLED BOTTLES.
#### (WHITE AND BUFF.) BASKETED IN WHITE WICKER.

Wickered to Shoulder.

| 2 qt. | 4 qt. | 6 qt. | 8 qt. | 12 qt. | 16 qt. | |
|---|---|---|---|---|---|---|
| 14/3 | 19/- | 24/- | 30/- | 47/- | 61/- | per doz. |

Wickered to Nose.

| 2 qt. | 4 qt. | 6 qt. | 8 qt. | 12 qt. | 16 qt. | |
|---|---|---|---|---|---|---|
| 17/3 | 23/- | 28/- | 34/- | 52/- | 67/- | per doz. |

Special Quotations given for large sizes of above.

Handled bottles, Denby Catalogue, 1909.

---

JOSEPH BOURNE & SON, DENBY POTTERY, NEAR DERBY.

Foot and hand-warmers, Denby Catalogue, 1909.

Tea and coffee pots, Denby Catalogue, 1907.

Special tableware was made for breakfast, luncheon, tea and dinner and the ware for each meal was advertised separately. An innovative teapot, the **S.Y.P.** in which the dome-shaped carrying-handle was fixed to the lid was made under patent in 1911. The letters stood for 'Simple Yet Perfect'.

**Emerald Ware** *on offer the same year, was glazed inside and out in green as a brighter alternative to Chocolate Ware and Brown and Green Ware.*

**Celeste**, *marketed in 1913, was different in style from Denby's utilitarian tableware designs. It was decorated in a warm cream-coloured slip with a broad blue band and bore a stencilled pattern in the art nouveau style.*

Celeste was to be the forerunner, by eighty years, of the superb decorative tableware that would be produced in the 1990s.

## DECORATIVE WARE

Horace Elliot continued to design for Denby and the blue and cream sgraffito mug with which he commemorated the success of his hero, Robert Baden-Powell, as the defender at the Siege of Mafeking in the Boer War, is preserved in the Denby Museum. He had a lengthy correspondence with the Powell family and presented a large version of the Denby commemorative mug to Baden-Powell. Following a similar theme, he created a three-handled punch-bowl in which each handle represented a famous naval gun – 'The Baden-Powell', 'The Nelson' and the 'The Skipping Sally'.

The high quality of Denby clay had been appreciated for many years and was supplied occasionally to other potteries. In 1909, the Martin Brothers, now at Southall,

approached Christopher Dale, the sales manager at Denby's showroom in London and it was arranged for Edwin Martin to visit Denby. Using Denby clay he created some decorative pieces which were successfully fired at Denby. He was so delighted with the result that he took some of the clay back to Southall where, unfortunately, it proved to be incompatible with the Martin Brothers' kiln.

Two examples of the work he produced at Denby were signed and dated 1909. A lidded pot bore the inscription 'C.J. Dale, October 1909, E.B. Martin, Denby' and a 4 ins. blue, grey and mauve vase was inscribed 'November 1909, Martin Brothers, Denby'. A magnificent vase depicting a large sinuous dragon was made out of Denby clay and almost certainly decorated by Edwin. Marked 'October 1909, Martin Brothers, London, Southall', it was cracked when taken from the Southall kiln and has since been owned by the Dale family.

The introduction of Denby art pottery was gradual and it was not until the 1920s that production achieved significant proportions. Whilst other factories such as Bretby, Lancastrian, Langley Mill, Royal Aller Vale and Watcombe were advertising and exhibiting art pottery, Denby's main pre-occupation was with bottles, household goods, cookware and kitchen ware. Decorative pottery was a subsidiary interest.

An insight into the development of the decorating department is given from lecture notes written in 1933 by Mr. R. Weston, who had worked at the Denby Pottery since the 1880s. Referring to the early years of the century he wrote that:

'An attempt was made during the time Mr. Horsley was manager to produce decorated ware, by means of

**Celeste** Tableware advertising leaflet. c.1913.

coloured slips. We had a Mr. Ridgway here, who had one or two of our young men with him. The decorations were butterflies, geese, flowers etc...There was a small aerograph with one hood, erected at this time, no great headway was made, and it was allowed to die down.'

**Butterfly Ware** *was an ephemeral, richly-coloured and finely hand-painted art pottery produced under the direction of Mr. Ridgway. Its bright blue glaze provided the mid-summer sky against which delicate butterflies and small birds flew above feathery green grasses.*

Market forces were indicating a new direction for expansion and diversification. Denby had always given priority to the manufacture of high-quality glazes, encouraging experimentation and the development of new techniques. In the early 1900s however, these skills were to be applied to decorative ware and combined with a new dynamic approach to colour. Gradually, an extensive repertoire of glazes was achieved, setting the stage for the brilliant art glazes that were to emerge so spectacularly in the 1920s.

In September 1904, *The Pottery Gazette* recorded that:

'They (Denby) have just brought out the 'Danesby' ware. This is a new colour scheme with mottled effects. It is applied to all tableware and also to art vases, flower pots etc.'.

This was actually a reference to a revival of art pottery rather than a new initiative as Danesby Ware was first mentioned in the magazine as early as 1886. Many flower tubes, vases and bulb bowls, in simple but pleasing shapes, were green-glazed and had little or no decoration other than a coloured glaze and occasional embossments. They were primarily functional and designed for the florist trade. In 1910, Denby was appointed sole manufacturer of the green **Blitz** flower holders, made in six sizes to fit Denby vases. A wider range of ornamental bulb bowls and fern pots, decorated with new glaze effects, was also presented in the same year.

**Vulcan Ware**, *named after a new metallic glaze, was one of the art glazes applied to vases, bulb bowls and novelty items including shoes, clogs and naturalistic animals such as pigs and frogs.*

Although a display of high-quality utilitarian Denby stoneware was praised when it was exhibited in Turin in 1911, the reporter in *The Pottery Gazette* wrote that:

'Among the highly decorative wares of other firms, this little stand appears somewhat of a Cinderella.'

Were Denby inspired or irritated by this article or would the ensuing developments in their art pottery have occurred in any event? Experiments in glaze techniques continued, leading to the introduction of high-quality, single-coloured art glazes in cobalt-blue, peacock-blue, myrtle-green, salmon-pink, emerald, celeste and heather-bloom. One *Pottery Gazette* of the period records that:

'It is really surprising what an extensive palette they (Denby) have been able to obtain on their unique body. There are few shades in self-coloured glazes that they are now not able to produce.'

Times were changing.

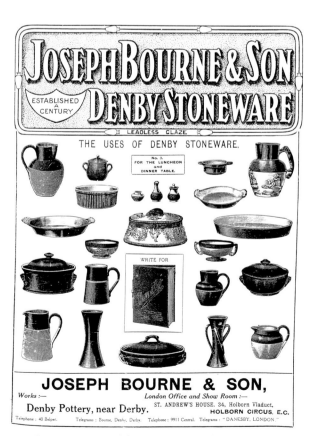

A selection of pre-World War I items, Denby Catalogue, 1911.

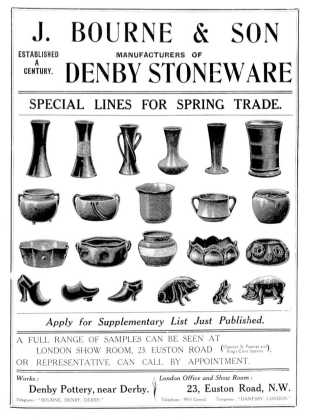

A selection of decorative ware, Denby Catalogue, 1908.

# CHAPTER 4

# AN ARCADIAN POTTERY
## 1916 - 1929

Despite the limitations imposed by wartime restrictions and the enlistment of many male staff, including Albert Colledge, Denby continued to prosper and became a limited company in 1916. Joseph Bourne-Wheeler was described as the Governing Director with George Horsley, Managing Director and Mrs. Florence Bourne-Wheeler the Company Secretary.

When the war ended in 1918, a commemorative Peace Celebration Mug was produced and Denby settled down to recover from the effects of the last four devastating years. Government work, taken on during the war, had seriously handicapped the firm and delayed deliveries. Twelve male staff had been killed in action and in common with most industrial firms the Pottery continued to employ even more women.

Despite the setbacks caused by the war, the firm had made considerable progress. When a reporter from *The Pottery Gazette* visited the London showrooms in 1919 he was invited by Alex Dale to go to Denby to see the improvements for himself. The following extract from a report dated 1st September 1919 gives a vivid contemporary impression of the situation in Denby at that time. The reporter obviously did not often venture into the provinces, except to visit Stoke-on-Trent, but found:

> '...that a fleet of motor 'buses now plies between Derby and Alfreton, serving the intermediate villages, and on most days of the week there is a 'bus every hour. These 'buses pass the very door of the Denby pottery, and consequently provide the best means of reaching the pottery from Derby. This method of transit was favoured by the writer of the present notes, and proved quite acceptable, by reason of the extremely pleasant

country through which one passes, particularly at the present time of year.

> On the occasion of one's first visit to Denby one is impressed by an atmosphere of rurality and antiquity about the place, in spite of evidences of much modern development at the pottery. Along the main road stand some fairly ancient cottages, whilst contiguous to the pottery is an old dwelling house, of a superior order, it is true, and now entailed by the factory to serve the purposes of its registered office, which seems to speak to one of the days of yore, when potting was conducted under much less exacting conditions than now, both industrially and commercially.'

(The 'ancient cottages' included 'The College', a family home of the Colledges, whilst the 'old dwelling house' was the former home of the Bourne family).

> 'The erection of a number of modern villas in the vicinity of Denby station have not effectually effaced the old time elements of the place; on the contrary, this has simply served to accentuate them. The village boasts of a grocer's shop, and a 'hotel'. The proprietor, one 'Potter' but only by name, makes no secret of the fact that he does not cater for the hungry, but only the thirsty, and ruthlessly directs the would-be diner to the next 'house' situated at Ripley, some three miles away...

> The first thing that appealed to me on arriving at the factory was the handsome modern frontage of the works, which was built, apparently to commemorate the firm's centenary ten years ago...It is at once apparent to the visitor that the original pottery, as a result of periodic modernisation, has been improved almost beyond recognition.

> The works cover, probably, eight or ten acres of land; they are replete with the latest machinery and time-saving devices; they are remarkably up-to-date considering they are so remotely situated from the main pottery-producing district of the country; and the fact that they normally employ some 500 hands all the year round goes to show that they are making those classes of goods...for which the demand is never flagging.

> ...I was conducted round the works by Mr. Hugh Horsley...We began at the very source, viz: – the clay mine, which is situated at the rear of the factory and quite close thereto. ...the Denby clay is actually mined, in contradistinction to being merely quarried. The clay is won on lines very similar to that in which the Dorset and Devon ball clays are worked, and is brought up from underground in wagons by means of an endless rope...On coming from the mine the clay is dumped into a weathering pit, where it is subjected for many months to the action of the weather...

Joseph Bourne-Wheeler, 1860-1942.

Florence Bourne-Wheeler, 1870-1948.

The College, family home of the Colledges.

The Bourne family home.

The Denby Pottery thus starts off with a wonderful advantage in having right at hand an abundant supply of really excellent clay, which, being won so close to the works, can be brought straight down from the weathering pit to the blunger by trolley...it is a particularly vitreous clay, which renders possible the manufacture of an excellent fire-proof ware, capable of withstanding sudden changes of temperature, as well as making possible the compounding of special bodies to withstand electric strains, acid corrosion etc... the clay, on leaving the storage pits passes along a gangway and on reaching the blunger is tipped directly into it, and passes from thence into a series of large slip tanks, capable of holding some 1,500 gallons of liquid clay. The subsequent lawning, filter-pressing and pugging is carried out very much on the same lines as at the majority of domestic potteries...the slip house is very extensive and thoroughly equipped, one such as many Staffordshire potters would be only too proud to possess.

The time saving devices...are as numerous as they are interesting. An endless elevator, for instance, conveys the prepared clay from the slip house on the ground floor to the clay-workers on the first floor, and the clay is taken from the elevator for the use of an army of throwers both male and female. I was particularly interested in the work of the girl throwers, some of whom were extremely youthful, but none the less capable. The smaller articles, such as cream jars, ointment jars, furniture cream containers, ink bottles, ginger beer bottles and the like, are practically all dealt with by girl labour, whilst the larger and more cumbersome pieces are handled by youths and men. The agility of the Denby throwers is a distinct feature of the place, and although I have seen many throwers from time to time, I can certainly say that I have never seen a more expeditious squad.

In successive order we visited the workrooms of the pressers, jolliers, and casters...particularly impressive was the array of foot-warmers, these being made by various processes and some of them printed with their distinctive names by means of an automatic Hassal roller-printing machine.

The foot-warmer is one of the firm's real specialities and I noticed in the course of my tour through the shops all the well known shapes...It is significant that summer and winter sees J. Bourne and Son Ltd., hard at work upon the manufacture of foot-warmers...

...(In the greenhouse) one was able to see huge quantities of ware undergoing the drying preparatory to the biscuit firing...It is situated midway between the respective potting departments so that the ware can be brought in from both ends. A tramway runs right through the greenhouse, so that the clay can be trolleyed in, and unnecessary handling and carrying can be obviated.

The biscuit firing of those wares which have subsequently to be fired for the glaze is done in a row of eight ovens which are constructed over the top of sixteen salt-glaze kilns, and the firing is achieved by means of the waste heat which leaves the latter...these particular ovens are commonly known on the works as The Canada's.

The dipping house into which the fired bisque ware passes, is, like the greenhouse, spacious and well-appointed...the dipping in its entirety, is done by...girl labour...When dipped the ware was transferred to an endless elevator, which has been erected during the war...all superfluous handling is avoided...the ware is

Another 'expeditious squad'.

Denby Pottery

not warehoused. It never lies about as it must unavoidably do at some factories but...passes out the same day as it enters.

The glost warehouses...are of tremendous extent. One of the principle of these is no less than 125 feet long by close upon 50 feet wide. This particular warehouse is reserved for domestic goods, separate bays being devoted to salt-glazed and electrical wares etc...all electrical insulators, of which the firm makes huge quantities, as well as of sparking plugs, are specially tested by methods approved by the Government departments which purchase them largely, and any defective insulator is immediately detected by the vagaries of a registering lamp.

Several main impressions seem to cling to me as a result of this tour to the Denby Pottery. First of all the homeliness and the apparent contentment of the workers, of whom quite a proportion are extremely youthful and of the gentler sex. I arrived at the works in the dinner hour, and it was refreshing to see the young workers frolicking about in the highway, skipping, cycling, jazzing and Tangoing to their hearts' content, concerned only with avoiding an occasional motor-car or motor cycle. Others lolled in the fields with which the works are surrounded whilst not a few reclined in deck chairs on the lawn in front of the office...

The healthy situation of the factory was my second chief impression...where one gets an unmistakable breeze even on a midsummer day such as that which I chose for my visit. No-one could fail to be impressed with the robustness and the strength of the young people employed at the pottery, both male and female.

One has only to watch the trousered girls in the vicinity of the ovens, carrying boards and saggars of ware, with free and easy gait, to see that far from prejudicing their health, their occupation in the village pottery is materially assisting in their development.

...a Welfare Committee has been established at the works, on which every department of the workers is represented, and this Committee now meets every month to consider all matters that arise affecting the welfare of the workers, and there appears to be

The warehouse, c.1919.

Workers in the top room, making small ware (those in the bottom room made large ware), c.1919.

An early photograph of crate makers at Denby Pottery.

evidence of hearty co-operation between employers and employed, who evidently recognise that their interests are mutual.

Lastly, the progressiveness of the house was unmistakably apparent...it is the obvious desire of the firm to be up-to-date in every way...

The factory has, of course, natural advantages by reason of its location, such as illimitable supplies of clay and coal, and an abundance of land on which to extend...they have to meet the disadvantages attendant upon the limitation of available labour, which they have to attract to the pottery from surrounding villages and train this labour by peculiar means to peculiar methods.

...it is really wonderful what J. Bourne and Son Ltd., have been able to accomplish up to now. There is nothing from the inartistic salt-glaze ink bottle up to the bright or matt glazed vase or flower pot which they do not produce and their range of household wares in Denby Stoneware is something that the dealer can conjure with. Their Chef Ware and fireproof goods have earned a legitimate reputation, and their green glaze and chocolate wares and teapots, coffee pots and allied articles need no introduction...Scores of miscellaneous lines, even to lemon squeezers and toast racks are found...'.

The situation described in this glowing report was to continue for at least the next decade with little change. Technical improvements made it possible to produce decorative pottery that had hitherto been thought impossible with stoneware clay. Administrative changes brought some of the clerical work back to Denby, thus freeing space for even larger showrooms. It was during the early 1920s that Joseph Wood was appointed Works Manager – he and his son Norman were to manage the firm for the next fifty-five years. One of Joseph's first decisions must have been to set up the decorating shop in 1923 to cater for the increase in decorative ware being produced. Albert Colledge was appointed to run the new department. With a young family, Albert must have been pleased by his promotion, even though, at first, his command consisted of only four young women decorators.

# THE DECORATIVE DIRECTION

A reporter from *The Pottery Gazette* of December 1915 indicated the esteem with which Denby was regarded in the pottery industry:

'Their London showrooms...are equipped with a range of samples such as every china and glass dealer, no matter whether situated in the most aristocratic neighbourhood of the city or in the remotest suburb must be glad to know of. Practicality seems to be the keynote of the production of the Denby pottery, for, although they are never seen in any form which involves exclusiveness in the matter of price, they are presented in many styles which are a close combination of utility and attractiveness, which in these days, means a good deal.'

These sentiments, albeit quaintly phrased, could equally well apply to the Denby pottery of today.

'One never thinks of this particular pottery without associating it with the manufacture of a type of household pottery which is a universal need...anything needed in the way of kitchen pottery or pottery requisites for the housekeeper is to think instinctively of Joseph Bourne and Son...From articles of strict utilitarian interest the productions of the Denby pottery have been steadily and effectively developed, until today, whether one requires articles of pottery for storage, culinary, or simple decorative purposes, the Denby line...(will) efficiently fill the need.'

Articles on display in the showroom in 1916 included bed-warmers, jars for cooking and storing – butter jars, covered brawn pots, covered bread pans, stew pots, cake pans, pickle jars, jelly cans, extract pots, preserve jars, round, oval and square baking dishes, hot pots, jelly moulds, bowls and lipped bowls. They were finished in three ways, as Brown Salt-glazed Ware, White and Buff Stoneware or as Light Stoneware.

Kitchen ware, Denby Catalogue, 1924.

Bed Time hot-water bottle.

Imagination and ingenuity were applied to the manufacture of hot-water bottles. A child's **Bed Time** hot-water bottle was made in the shape of a six-sided clock on which the fingers pointedly reinforced an eight o' clock bed time. On the same theme, the **Little Folks** bed-warmer with its illustration of a child pulling back the bedclothes and slipping into bed enticed children throughout the 1920s to climb 'the wooden hill to Bedfordshire'.

Towards the end of the 1920s the range was extended to include two examples modelled to imitate handbags complete with leather carrying-handles. **The Boudoir** in a bright, mottled blue with a brown 'frame' was decorated with a picture of a lady in a boudoir cap, whilst the other brown handbag bore the initials, 'B.E.D.' emblazoned on the front with a label humorously indicating 'Passenger To The Land Of Nod' – a message that was to be repeated until the outbreak of World War II.

Brown Fireproof, Green Fireproof and Chef Cookware together with Denby Ware, Chocolate Ware and Emerald Ware were on offer throughout the period.

In 1928 Denby's new **Blue Flame Casserole** was glazed in traditional brown, green, Cottage Blue and a new walnut-brown. The casserole had a hollowed base which enabled the heat from a small flame to be distributed evenly throughout, and for the heat to be conserved and circulated between the outer and inner casing of the container. This ensured that the food cooked evenly as if it had been cooked inside the oven, not on top of it. Most economical to use, it was direct evidence of the constant upgrading of Denby cookware and the improvement in efficiency achieved by good design and innovation. The constant progression, attention to detail and awareness of their customers' requirements enabled the firm to become increasingly successful throughout the 1920s.

In the post-war years, tableware was gradually enlivened by new, more brightly-coloured glazes.

**Mahogany Ware** *was traditionally glazed in a new rich brown.*

**Celeste** *marketed at the same time, was glazed in two shades of blue. On each pot the smooth, dark, upper part was separated from its roughened, light-blue base by a line of beading. It should not be confused with the earlier art nouveau styled tableware of the same name.*

**Cottage Blue Ware**, *with its rich blue mottled glaze and yellow interior, was quite different from the soft browns and greens of earlier tableware. Introduced in 1926, on traditional shapes, its distinctive blue glaze remained a favourite with successive generations.*

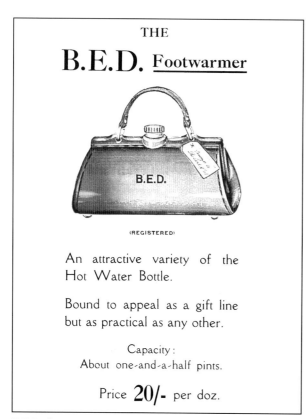

B.E.D. foot-warmer advertisement, late 1920s.

Blue Flame Casserole, Denby Catalogue, 1930.

Coloured glaze tableware, Denby Catalogue, 1930.

Patented teapots, Denby Catalogue, 1932.

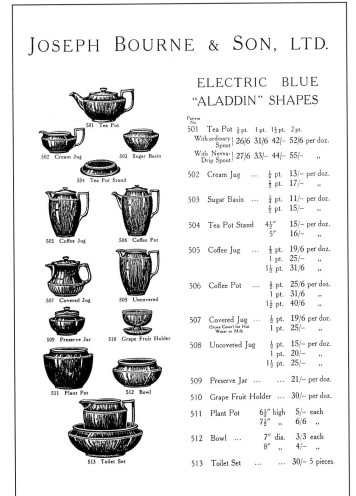

**Electric Blue Aladdin** tableware, Denby Catalogue, 1930.

**Saffron Ware** *was brightly glazed in shades of yellow. Issued in the same year as the typically English Cottage Blue, it had an affinity with the French pie-crust type of kitchen ware.*

**Electric Blue**, *an original art glaze was, by the latter part of the 1920s, enhancing a new series of tableware shapes inspired by Aladdin's lamp. Although this influence was apparent in the outline of the teapot, the real 'magic' was in the blue glaze.*

Denby continued to improve the functional as well as the decorative aspects of its tableware. A series of innovatory teapots was marketed: The **Nevva-Drip** of 1922 with its faultless pouring spout (later to be applied to many other teapots); **The Pekoe** of 1929 with spoutless shape, lock-lid and sunken knob (especially appropriate for the catering trade because of its safety and space saving features).

Innovation was to the forefront of design.

## DECORATIVE WARE

Denby's gradual development and increasing use of decorative coloured glazes was beginning to make a distinct impression in the world of ceramics. New shapes, glazes and ornamentation proclaimed the firm's commitment to the manufacture of pottery that was specifically designed to have aesthetic appeal. Colourful art glazes including matt glazes in green, pink, mauve, and heliotrope, were applied to decorative ware and to toilet sets. Vases, matt-glazed in black were issued in 1917, perhaps to commemorate the many individual wartime tragedies.

It was not until the 1920s that Denby became recognised as a serious contender in the arena of art pottery. Initially, reports in trade magazines reminded readers that Denby pottery was one in which novelty and decoration were subordinate to utility and that there were:

'...no rabid alterations from season to season. All that is noted is a quiet, gradual, persistent growth to something better.'

Stoneware produced from Denby clay was ideal for utilitarian domestic ware, as over one hundred years of experience had proved. However, it was not the most amenable material from which to develop what was to become Denby's unique art pottery. As the potters perfected their new craft, Denby assumed an increasingly high profile in the market for decorative ware. Denby had been likened to an enormous studio pottery and it cannot be emphasised too strongly that as all the ware was hand-crafted, each piece was unique. Scientific and technological developments had made it possible to produce more decorative and aesthetically pleasing stoneware. Not only was the ware durable and splendidly hand-thrown but experiments in glaze techniques and the introduction of new coloured glazes and decoration was elevating Denby stoneware into the category of art pottery.

As early as 1920 *The Pottery Gazette* records that:

'A new line of Danesby art ware was shown in a tone of electric blue broken up with an interesting sort of mottling. This particular range includes many attractive small vases all hand thrown on the wheel.'

Five years later Electric Blue was presented as a major decorative series.

The year 1923 was a turning point in the production of Denby art pottery as it was the year in which Albert Colledge was promoted to take charge of the decorating shop. From then onward Denby art pottery developed its own distinct identity, being displayed at Wembley in the British Empire Exhibition of 1924.

From a lecture given by Mr. Weston in the decorating shop in 1933 we learn that the shop had been specially built about ten years previously, and that:

'Tube lining filled in with glaze now became very popular. Electric Blue has had a great time. Orient and Pastel Ware are very much liked. This department has grown very steadily and is producing a good quantity of superior decorative ware, which is a valuable asset to the firm. I should say that this department has a great future before it, as it is very young compared to the rest of the works.'

**Tube-Lined Danesby Ware** *in 1923 consisted of a range of narrow-necked vases, bowls and jardinières each of which was decorated with a band of stylised rosettes.*

*A second series was based on individually named hand-thrown shapes in plain or mottled, matt or glossy art glazes – Royal Blue, Matt Blue, Electric Blue, Electric Green, and Pewter. Each bore a precise, tube-lined decoration. The windmill, which featured on Denby's early sprigged ware, made*

*a scenic appearance and gradually floral designs reflected the sinuous lines of the art nouveau style.*

**Persian Style Danesby Ware**, *magnificent in a rich dark-brown, was tube-lined with freely drawn Persian-styled flowers and leaves. These rustic-shaped vases had hidden depths as it was not until they were struck by sunlight that the true brilliance of the clove-pink, turquoise, cobalt-blue flowers and green leaves was revealed.*

*The Pottery Gazette* of September 1925 confirms that:

'Denby Pottery have made conspicuous headway on the artistic side of their domestic stoneware production during the last few years. Ever since the institution at Denby of the new 'Danesby' series of decorated stoneware, the artistic succession seems to have been unbroken...The production of the 'Danesby' ware may be regarded as having marked an epoch in the history of the Denby firm...whilst no one had ever questioned the technical merit of Denby stoneware, the artistic side had yet to be largely explored.'

The contribution of Albert Colledge at this time was crucial, and from his son Glyn we learn of Albert's direct involvement, almost certainly with the production of the Electric Blue range and definitely in the creation of Orient Ware. Glyn owns one of his father's prototypes of Orient Ware.

**Electric Blue Ware** *refers to a magnificent series of jugs, vases and bowls most of which were specially designed to display the strikingly original glaze. Marketed in 1925 as Danesby Electric Blue Ware it was such a success that the range of shapes was later extended. The Danesby stamp, the original of which was hand-written by Albert Colledge, was added to this design and subsequently to other Danesby art ware.*

**Roman Ware** *consisted of vases decorated in red, brown, purple, green and other coloured glazes, superimposed on a grey ground. It was likened to old Roman pottery in The Pottery Gazette of 1926.*

**Orient Ware** *captured the public's imagination with its unique glazes. The matt, crystalline glaze in mauve and brown shaded into and complemented the rich, deep blue, matt glaze on the body of each pot. It adorned new shapes and some of those used for the Electric Blue range.*

Denby art pottery was now established. *The Pottery Gazette* of April 1927 wrote:

'Denby Pottery is capable of producing today stoneware that is able to fill a role in every room of the house. At one time it was thought that stoneware was only suitable for the kitchen, but that idea is, apparently, now once and for all time exploded.'

The following year Danesby was exhibited at the Victoria and Albert Museum and at the British Industries Fair. A reporter from *The Pottery Gazette* summed up Denby's contribution to the trade fair as being:

'Unquestionably the finest and most impressive which the firm has ever made at a public exhibition, and to say that is to say much.'

# CHAPTER 5

# SURVIVAL AND REVIVAL
# 1930 - 1945

In common with the rest of the pottery industry, Denby experienced the effects of the world's economic depression in the 1930s. By 1930 its shareholders were receiving no dividends, workers' wages were cut and even senior staff such as Alex Dale, who ran the London showroom, were having to make personal economies. His son John was at boarding school but had to be brought home because his parents could no longer afford the fees. Consequently, John started work at Denby, at first in a very junior capacity. In 1931 another young man, Norman Wood, joined the firm as an assistant works manager.

Under Norman Wood's management, Denby survived the Depression. One of the first improvements made, soon after his appointment in 1931, was the replacement of the old beehive kilns by the more efficient Dressler tunnel ovens. At the same time he turned his attention to the current range of products and decided that new designs were needed if sales were to be increased. Consequently, he encouraged the policy of recruiting freelance designers of the highest calibre.

## DONALD GILBERT

One such designer was the thirty year old sculptor Donald Gilbert whose skilfully modelled birds and animals soon enlivened Denby's decorative range. The son of a sculptor, Walter Gilbert, Donald was born in Burcot, Worcestershire and trained in Birmingham and at the Royal College of Art in London. His tutor in London was the famous Sir Alfred Gilbert who designed the statue of Eros that now stands in Piccadilly Circus.

Donald's distinguished background was reflected in the quality of his work for Denby. Recognised as minor works of art, his animal figures were purchased by Queen Mary and the Duke of Kent. Whilst the Queen chose a pair of his elephant bookends, the Duke is said to have taken the full range of Donald Gilbert's animals for the young Prince Edward. His work was equally popular with many of Denby's customers who also appreciated the classic lines of his oven-to-tableware designs. By the end of the decade, after successful exhibitions of his sculptures in the mid-1930s, he appears to have severed his connection with the Pottery. It was about this time that Horace Elliott also broke his long association with the firm.

## ALICE TEICHTNER

Continuing the policy of recruiting new designers, Denby introduced a continental influence in 1936 in the person of Alice Teichtner, an Austrian artist. Alice Teichtner was born in Vienna on 6th July 1896. After working for the Schwadron brothers, she took part in the internationally renowned Wiener Werkstatte (Vienna Workshop) which was founded in 1903 to make and sell the best in modern design and craftsmanship. Its aim was to re-unite form and function and to create 'total works of art' as envisaged by John Ruskin and William Morris, two of the founders of the British Arts and Crafts movement.

During the mid-1920s Alice set up her own studio in Vienna and like her famous contemporary, Lucie Rie, attended the Kunstgewerbeschule (Art Trade School). Her work was illustrated in the *British Studio Year Book of Decorative Art* in 1924 and in *The Pottery Gazette* of the same year. Incidentally, Denby records show that Lucie Rie was to use Denby clay for the creation of some of her internationally renowned pottery.

When the Nazis gained power in Germany and Austria in the 1930s many artists of Jewish origin sought asylum in Britain. It is possible that Alice Teichtner met the Bourne-Wheelers when they were on one of their continental holidays but, whatever the reason, she left Austria and joined Denby Pottery. With her distinctive style of studio pottery she made a great impact at Denby contributing many striking designs.

Although she was fluent in French, Alice's command of English was limited. Nevertheless, she was able to convey her ideas to her Denby colleagues when she emerged from the small studio she had been given by Norman Wood. The Denby workers were rather in awe of this formidable Austrian woman with her imposing presence, overwhelming enthusiasm and loud, guttural voice. There was also an element of suspicion and xenophobia, particularly amongst those who remembered the First World War. Despite this, Alice was respected for her undoubted talent and knowledge of ceramics. She amused the workers by her lack of deference towards Denby's management – she would shout 'Florence!' to attract the attention of Florence Bourne-Wheeler as she made her dignified way through the factory.

Alice Teichtner's designs, Vienna c.1924.

Alice lived at the historic Denby Hall Farm which has since been demolished to make way for open-cast coal mining. When the war with Germany broke out in 1939 she had to register as an alien. Wartime restrictions soon meant that the Pottery was not able to use her talents and, in 1943, she decided to emigrate to Canada.

## NEW DEVELOPMENTS

In the year of King George V's Silver Jubilee, 1935, the London showroom was remodelled. A contemporary photograph in a trade magazine showed a design that would not appear out-of-date today. Curved shelves and display stands were complemented with chromium plated tables and chairs, the latter upholstered in scarlet. In the same article, an illustration of the new Burgess and Leigh showroom, furnished in a conventional style, demonstrated what a striking effect the Denby designers had achieved. By that time John Dale would have joined his father Alex in London and may well have had a modernising influence.

On leaving school in 1938, Albert Colledge's younger son, Glyn, joined him as an apprentice modeller to begin what was to develop into a distinguished career. By then

Norman Wood had visionary plans for the development of the Pottery but the impending war kept them on the drawing board.

Denby was not one of the potteries privileged to export during the war and had to confine itself to the manufacture of plain ware and industrial products for the war effort. Many of the staff enlisted, including Glyn Colledge. During the war, on the last day of 1942, Joseph Bourne-Wheeler died. His place as Chairman of the company was taken by his widow, Florence, and that of Governing Director by Norman Wood's father, Joseph.

Possibly as a reward for its contribution to the war effort, Denby's plans for reconstruction were agreed by the Government in 1943. Work could not commence immediately but Norman Wood had envisaged a grand design to project the outdated factory into the post-war world. As the war neared its end, however, the company was able to open a new works canteen where the employees were entertained from time to time by live performances of the B.B.C.'s *Workers' Playtime*. In 1944, Eileen White, a future Director and Company Secretary, joined the company as an office junior.

# BEAUTY COMBINED WITH UTILITY

**M Pyre Chef Ware**, Denby Catalogue, 1932.

Throughout the 1930s cooking ware and tableware remained the backbone of Denby's production. **Quaker Brown** was a variation of the old Denby Brown and Cottage Blue appeared, most aptly, under a new advertising slogan, 'Beauty Combined with Utility'. This statement coincided appropriately with the appointment of a freelance designer, Donald Gilbert, whose work proved to be a major factor in determining the direction in which Denby Pottery was to advance.

In 1931 he transformed the lowly hot-water bottle when he modelled **Wilfred The Hot Water Rabbit** as a free-standing, stylised rabbit together with a squirrel and a

penguin, each comfortingly decorated in traditional brown, blue or green Denby glazes. He created two other warmers, one embossed with a cat eyeing a mouse, and the other with a pair of curled dormice.

1933 was a productive and significant year. The needs of pets were catered for by a proliferation of named CAT and DOG food bowls in many shapes, sizes and coloured glazes. Kitchen storage jars received a new modern treatment. Banded in the bright green popular in the 1930s they were individually labelled with a tube-lined inscription of their contents.

Brown and Green Fireproof cooking ware remained in service unchanged but Chef Ware was updated, with the traditional Chef Ware marketed as M-Pyre Chef Ware to emphasise the world-wide market which Denby supplied.

**M-Pyre Chef Ware** *was partly glazed outside and fully glazed inside in an amber colour.*

**M-Pyre Bramber Ware**, *fully glazed in brown and amber followed in 1935.*

**M-Pyre Apex Ware**, *first made in 1937, had an unglazed exterior with a red lid and interior.*

**Medici Decorative Fireproof Ware** *was made exclusively for the Medici Society in 1937. It was glazed in white with pale-blue or brown hand-painted leaf sprays, arranged diagonally around the pot.*

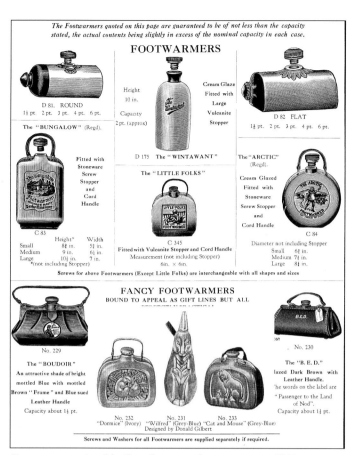

Factory promotional leaflet advertising foot-warmers, c.1931.

Animal feeding bowls, Denby Catalogue, 1932.

**Brown, White and Buff Stoneware**, Denby Catalogue, 1937.

**Brown, White and Buff Stoneware**, Denby Catalogue, 1937.

**Brown Stoneware** (black glazed top) for decoration and utility, Denby Catalogue, 1937.

Jelly moulds, Denby Catalogue, 1937.

Although the output of traditional oven and tableware was maintained, the product was revitalised by striking new glazes and the designs of Donald Gilbert.

**Sterling Cooking Ware**, *introduced in dark mahogany with a light stone interior, was in the old style.*

**Epic**, *based on Donald Gilbert's classic shapes, was glazed in a subtle myrtle-green with cream-lined interiors and simple, distinctive, incised scalloped decoration. First produced in 1933, it was named after its glaze which became a recognised Denby colour.*

**Blue Cone** *oven and tableware, designed in 1937 by Donald Gilbert made a direct appeal to modern taste with its ivory and blue colourway. The addition of a decorative, hand-painted blue fir cone represented a major change of policy.*

These two designs proved to be a turning point in Denby's future approach to the production of oven and tableware. The emphasis was to be not only on function but directly on the quality of design and aesthetic appeal.

**Manor Green,** *named after its new glaze, was based on rounded oven-to-tableware shapes designed by Donald Gilbert in 1938/9. Manor Green became a classic in the Denby palette.*

Denby was producing simultaneously, and with success, designs in the traditional and the modern idiom.

Promotion of the **Nevva-Drip** teapot in a variety of shapes and glazes, continued throughout the decade before being superseded in 1939 by the new **Stop Drip** which was patented and applied to teapots, coffee pots and jugs.

Two series of domestic stoneware consisting mainly of different sized jugs, together with a set of plain functional flower vases, were issued during the 1930s.

**Brown Stoneware** *with the upper part of each piece glazed in black, was limited to jugs, bowls, mugs, a cider set and a toilet set.*

**Redstone,** *made of terracotta clay with unglazed exterior and glazed interior, had a similar range of items but included a selection of bulb bowls.*

**Greenstone** *vases and jugs were thickly potted and glazed in matt green. The pitted surface was reminiscent of old hammered ware.*

Because of wartime restrictions, coloured domestic ware was gradually phased out and throughout most of the wartime years, Denby was allowed to produce industrial ware only and a limited supply of utility articles for the domestic market. The latter were either glazed in the mahogany brown that had been first introduced after World War I, or in plain brown. A new item in the catalogue, a ceramic surround for an electric fire, was an innovation born of the necessity to replace scarce metals.

# DECORATIVE WARE

During the 1930s attention was focused on the production of prestigious, high-quality ornamental ware until the advent of World War II halted production. Freelance designers, Donald Gilbert and Alice Teichtner, determined the way in which Danesby Ware was to develop in the 1930s.

Danesby Ware was created by a group of artists and craftspeople each of whom played a vital role. The in-house designers drew on the accumulated knowledge of the chemists and technicians who created the glaze effects, and on the skill and experience of the modellers, hand-throwers and decorators.

With this combined expertise Denby was able to compete successfully with the decorative ware being produced by the prolific Stoke-on-Trent potteries which utilised the far more easily worked earthenware clay. Danesby Ware was an artistic and technical achievement. Effects were achieved in stoneware that no-one had previously believed possible. Electric Blue and Orient Ware retained their popularity and a set of ashtrays, modelled in 1930 by Henry Litton in the shape of the four playing-card suits, was added to the Orient Ware range.

Denby was justifiably renowned for the high-quality reactive glazes which its chemists created with such skill and flair. To build on the success of the blue Danesby Ware, comparable designs using green art-glazes were introduced in 1930.

**Electric Green** *echoed in green the art glaze of Electric Blue. Produced on a very limited scale it was applied to some selected shapes from the original series.*

**Meadow Green** *in soft lustrous green, was applied to some of the Orient Ware shapes.*

**Antique Green**, *named to reflect the quality of its glaze, consisted of finely hand-thrown vases, jugs and bowls bearing a broad continuous band of brown, arabesque-styled tube-lining. Albert Colledge was responsible for the decoration and finish.*

Other decorative art glazed ware followed.

**Silver Grey**, *a robust, roughly-textured series, was listed in the Denby archives of 1931. One version was decorated in dark-blue with a simple scrolled or Greek Key pattern band, whilst another version displayed bold geometric designs infilled with a dark-brown glaze. Pieces are to be found stamped 'Denby Grey'.*

**Moorland**, *on new shapes and on some from the Electric Blue range, was encircled by a simple, incised stylised leaf or geometric decoration, and was richly glazed in merging earth colours, ochre, ivory, green and brown.*

**Florentine** *was also recorded in 1932 as a new art glaze series.*

Experiments were made with lustre glazes but it was the subtle matt glazes which gradually gained ascendence.

# DONALD GILBERT

An artist and sculptor, Donald Gilbert ensured that animals and birds were translated into Denby clay either as free-standing models or sculpted onto pots. Many of his animals reflecting the current art deco and modernist styles of the period, achieved a simplicity of line which succeeded in capturing the essence of the creatures. It was as a result of his enthusiasm that so many animals left the Denby factory with style and perennial appeal.

**Animal Ware** *by Donald Gilbert displayed stylised animals and birds. In 1931 penguins paraded on matt-glazed, parchment-coloured vases, and free-standing kingfishers and lovebirds perched on bowls whilst bookends, the epitomè of 1930s design, featured sculptured cats, dogs, lovebirds and pelicans.*

Donald Gilbert's enthusiasm for sculpture and animals created a veritable Noah's Ark at Denby. Fish as ornaments, on bookends and ashtrays, fluttering birds, a drake, three geese and small groups of lambs and rabbits were decorated in Danesby Pastel colours. Donald Gilbert modelled many of the stylised animals but the range was continually extended throughout the 1930s with pieces designed by Albert Colledge and Alice Teichtner. They were decorated in a variety of art glazes including Electric Blue, Orient, Silver Grey and, in 1939, Manor Green.

**Danesby Pastel** *introduced in 1933, was originally matt-glazed in two colourways. Many of the distinctive jugs and bowls were embossed with flowers, trees, birds and animals such as a giraffe, an antelope and a fawn. The bold, simplified flowers and the animals standing against a background of stylised trees indicate not only the influence of the art deco period but the hand of Donald Gilbert. Each shape was named after a town or village in the English Lake District.*

**Regent Pastel** *was glazed in subtle shades of cream, brown and green.*

**Pastel Blue** *was issued simultaneously in pastel shades with blue predominating.*

**Sylvan Pastel**, *marketed in 1935 on a limited number of the original Danesby Pastel shapes, was matt-glazed in soft shades of green.*

**Herbaceous Border** *created the effect of shrubs and trees by the effective use of sponge decoration in green and blue set against a grey background. The decoration, by Albert Colledge, was placed on Electric Blue and Orient Ware shapes.*

**Garden Ware** *was a variation on the sylvan theme. In 1934 Donald Gilbert's animals were arranged in a spectacular display of garden ornaments at the Olympia Exhibition Centre, London. His penguins, ducks, geese, frogs and squirrels, were placed in a natural setting complete with trees, shrubs, crazy-paving, a fountain and a running stream.*

# ALICE TEICHTNER

The designs of Alice Teichtner added an extra dimension to the Danesby range. She was an extraordinary woman who was an artist first and foremost and who had some difficulty in conforming to commercial constraints. The qualities of Denby stoneware and techniques were ideally suited to her vigorous and highly original talents. Alice Teichtner's work was unmistakable, her pots heavy, their colours muted. Her unconventional attitudes were reflected in her designs.

Highly energetic and directly involved with the pottery, she would stand by the throwers issuing her instructions and advice in a strong German accent. Her work was thrown by Bernard Fretwell who was responsible for throwing all the really large pieces at Denby, and by Cecil Wingfield. Charles Cresswell was her figure-man.

Technically skilled and knowledgeable about glazes, she doled out and mixed her own colours by instinct rather than by exact measurements. She used a scoop from a set of scales to achieve the correct proportion of basic materials, and a thimble to select the underglaze stains, oxides and glaze stains. At this time, and indeed until as late as 1947/48, glaze-colouring oxides in use included copper, cobalt, chrome, manganese, iron, titanium and rutil.

Some of Alice Teichtner's designs for Denby are well documented whilst others may be considered to be her work, or partly her work, by virtue of style and period of production. An undocumented series of large, heavy jugs, simply glazed in muted shades of ochre, with bold spiral embossments, may well fall into the latter category.

**Noah's Ark** by Donald Gilbert, c.1930.

Denby Pottery

 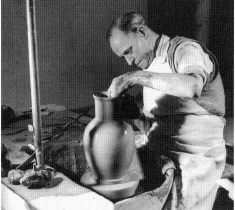 

Bernard Fretwell, thrower.　　Cecil Wingfield, thrower.　　Lambs being cast at the Pottery, c.1940.

**Featherstone** *was the ware she designed to extend the original Pastel Range. Strong and robust, with a simple applied decoration of stylised flowers and leaves, the shapes were named after Scottish towns and villages. It was matt-glazed in colours similar to those used for the original series.*

**Greenland** *exhibited similar characteristics but the embossments which included a pine cone, dandelion clocks and serrated leaves were bolder, larger, and set against a matt snow-white ground. It was almost certainly designed by Alice Teichtner or, at the very least, directly influenced by her.*

**Tyrolean Ware,** *issued in 1937, displayed her stamp, AT, usually painted underglaze in cobalt-blue. Tyrolean was matt-glazed in old gold, or in sepia enhanced by either blue or gold. Within the series the overall style was maintained but with variations. Some shapes were sculptural with an over-riding strength and power. Ornamentation consisted of prominent handles, a simple, crimped strip to emphasise a curve, and minimal scenes implied using a few modelled lines. A floral theme was developed in which spiky flowers were moulded onto the surface of a vase or it was adorned with a realistically modelled circlet or bunch of berries and leaves. Shallow bowls in the shape of a water-lily were composed of individually modelled petals.*

**Floral Pastel** *was richly embossed with naturalistic flowers, foxgloves, fuschia, marguerites, anemones, hollyhocks and Canterbury Bells. Set against a pale-grey ground they were modelled and positioned to enhance the boldly-shaped, hand-thrown vases and jugs. Denby's chief exponents at the time were Alice Teichtner and Albert Colledge. It is likely that she designed the shapes, and he the decoration, in 1937/38.*

**Gretna** and **Farmstead** *were two of the most restrained Danesby designs which relied on the quality of form and glaze for their attraction. Two colourways were applied to the same series of vigorous, yet austere, shapes. Gretna was glazed in a soft, light-green with contrasting dark-green edge and handles, and Farmstead had a semi-bright ivory background, highlighted by blue edging and handles. They are believed to be by Alice Teichtner for the following reasons: firstly, because of the bold shapes and general style; secondly, because of a spiral decoration which she also used on a Tyrolean bowl; thirdly,*

*because Gretna is a Scottish name as were others chosen for Featherstone. Denby advertised the two series proudly:*

> 'All the shapes show the mind of the artist whose aim is to produce something not only beautiful but practical and of a colour not likely to clash with the most subtle scheme of decoration.'

The advertisement went on to explain the priority Denby gave to good form:

> 'What is good form?...It means good design – the first essential of which is 'Fitness for purpose'. The ideal vase or bowl should depend upon form as much as colour and decoration for its effect.'

**Folkweave,** *designed immediately before the war, is believed to have resulted from the co-operation of Alice Teichtner and Albert Colledge; she producing typically strong shapes, and he the decoration in which textured, criss-crossed lines were stippled in soft pastel shades and in browns.*

## ALBERT COLLEDGE

Albert Colledge continued his valuable work in the art ware department, making a significant contribution to design and decoration.

**Ivory Pastel** *was highly decorative and genuinely pretty. Designed by Albert, the profusely clustered yellow flowers with green stems and leaves were relief-modelled by Hedley Parkin and set against a brown stippled ground.*

**Ripple,** *issued in 1936, was the first of a series of modern-styled decorative pottery which he introduced. Its horizontally-ridged, cream surface with contrasting green interior was not typical of Denby stoneware, having more in common with similar ware currently being made at the potteries of Stoke-on-Trent.*

**Old Ivory** *was a comparatively simple series of horizontally-ridged shapes, matt-glazed in ivory and issued in 1939.*

**Waverley** *also designed by Albert Colledge in the same year, made a direct appeal to modern taste and was advertised as:*

> 'A new range of vases introducing the best features of a traditional period produced by modern artists. In delightful self colours – Cream – Pale Green – Dusky Pink etc.'

**Byngo** and friends, an exhibition photograph, c.1940.

## GLYN COLLEDGE

Glyn, working with his father, was given the opportunity to create his first set of Danesby ware which was, incidentally, one of the last pre-war designs.

**Old English, Spring Time, Cottage** and **Tibet** *were a series of simple vases and jugs by Glyn with one version of Old English decorated with two modelled flowers and leaves. With the exception of the unusual brown running-glazes shading into blue, chosen by Albert Colledge for Tibet, the ware was glazed in pastel shades.*

## NOVELTY ITEMS

As the range of Danesby Ware increased so did the number of novelties, new items often appearing with a new Danesby series. The origins of one Denby favourite, **Marmaduke** the rabbit, are shrouded in mystery. Barbara Wood told the authors that Mrs. Bourne-Wheeler had said that it was on one of their continental holidays that she and her husband had found the original of Marmaduke. Marmaduke proliferated in typical rabbit fashion and is to be found in seven sizes ranging from just over one inch to 'doorstop'. He was also marketed as **Cottontail**, a tail-less cottonwool container.

His rival in the popularity stakes was **Byngo** the bulldog who was reproduced in five sizes and who viewed the world from button-black eyes with an appealing 'lost'

expression. He is most usually found in cream, brown or green but always with a dark left ear. Like all Denby animals, he was a weighty creature.

Alice Teichtner demonstrated her versatility when she modelled a realistic version of Norman Wood's Scottie dog and a quintet of terriers, at the same time caricaturing an appealing **Fido** reproduced in four, doleful sizes. Dachshunds multiplied minimally and hounds, by Albert Colledge, ran vainly in pursuit of a fox, as cute puppies appealed to new young owners.

When war started in September 1939 a flock of **Lambs** in cream and pale turquoise-green, with only the occasional black sheep, was loosed on the British public. An extensive catalogue of novelties included: a sea-lion, a teddy bear, an elephant, an A.R.P. dog; ashtrays sporting a footballer, a golfer and a skier; seagulls perching on bookends, a squirrel sitting on a marmalade pot and, everywhere, the ubiquitous bunnies, decorated in a wide variety of glazes. They appeared solo, on bookends, in twos by a group of toadstools, and in threes on ashtrays. In October 1945 an advertisement illustrating a Denby rabbit caged behind a wire fence had a message for the British public:

> 'Poor bunny has been penned up for six years. Not much longer now. Soon we're hoping to let him go and then he'll be finding his way into all the shops in the country. There's a Benjamin and Peter and Flopsy, Mopsy and Cotton-tail; the whole family in a range of colourful finishes. Yes, Denby artware is really coming back.'

Rabbit advertising poster, c.1945.

**Byngo** advertising poster, c.1945.

Giraffe advertising poster, c.1945.

# CHAPTER 6

# THE WOODS AND DALES OF DENBY

Norman Wood, 1909-1985.

For a rural company, Denby's senior staff could not have been more appropriately named – Bourne, Wood and Dale – although there was nothing bucolic about their efficiency as managers. The Bourne family history has already been outlined, ending with the death of Joseph Bourne-Wheeler in 1942 whilst the Woods and the Dales flourished from the Pottery's early days to the 1970s.

## THE WOODS

The first member of the Wood family to work at Denby was Joseph Wood who joined as a wages clerk in 1893 at the age of sixteen. Each Friday he would cycle with the workers' wages to the company's sister Pottery at Eastwood. If it was raining, he would cycle under his raised umbrella. Joseph progressed to the post of Works Manager by 1920 when he succeeded George Horsley and, when Joseph Bourne-Wheeler died in 1942, he became Managing Director. When T.G. Rawlings died in 1949, Joseph was made Company Chairman. He held this office until his own death in 1960 in his eighty-fourth year.

Unlike his father, Norman Douglas Wood was trained for management. At first he enrolled at the North Staffordshire College of Technology to learn the technology of ceramics. He is said to have been a brilliant pupil who led his class every year.

It was planned that he should go to the United States to continue his training but a lecture on the theory of management given by Dr. Bowie of the Dalton Hall College of Technology in Manchester University convinced him that he should transfer to that institution. By the time he left Manchester he was well equipped to take up a management post in Denby.

When he joined Denby Pottery at the age of twenty-two, in 1931, the firm was in the grip of the worldwide Depression, working a three-day week and paying no dividends. With his father, he set about modernising the Pottery, recruiting designers and generally applying all the skills he had acquired in Stoke-on-Trent and Manchester. As an aspiring manager he was impatient of his father's 'open-door' style of management. Joseph was happy to talk to any member of the staff who came to his office but Norman felt that it was inefficient to allow his concentration to be distracted in this way.

Norman's commitment to Denby Pottery was said to be legendary. He would always clock on at the same time as his staff and, during the war, worked seven days a week. The enlistment of staff created so many vacancies that Norman devised a scheme for recruiting staff wives on nominal wages to fill the gaps. Norman's own wife Barbara was no exception. After a spell on the Pottery floor, in designer overalls from John Lewis, she found herself in charge of personnel work and the canteen. An Oxford graduate, Barbara Wood eventually became Company Secretary and an influential Director.

Norman Wood was involved in every aspect of the company's work and played a significant part in influencing designs, glazes and techniques as well as general management. Albert Colledge is said to have remarked, 'Percy Hunt (the firm's chemist) thinks

Barbara Wood.

Norman's a chemist, Victor Thompson (the factory engineer) think he's an engineer, I know he's an artist.'

In complete contrast to John Dale's 'hail fellow, well met' style, he was a serious, modest, quietly spoken man who could negotiate firmly with staff and colleagues. He was also an authority on stoneware, as a lecture reproduced in the 1938 *Pottery Gazette* confirms. New designs would be brought home for his wife to try out in the kitchen or dining room and even his pet Scottie dog was enlisted as a model.

His personal taste was for the pure lines of Scandinavian design but he recognised the need to satisfy the popular market. Nevertheless, the designers he recruited reflected his own austere taste. Committed to contemporary design principles they were at the top of their profession and included Kenneth Clark and Tibor Reich. Norman was quick to spot new talent and when John Dale drew his attention to the outstanding work of a student, Gill Pemberton, he recognised her potential and recruited her. He sought to influence the work of his in-house designers – Albert and Glyn Colledge who developed the Denby look, and Alice Teichtner who pursued her own, highly individual course.

When the factory was reconstructed after the war, Norman Wood acted as Clerk of Works to keep close control of the changes. The resultant renovation was widely praised in the trade press and made for even more efficient production. Joseph Bourne-Wheeler saw Norman as his eventual successor.

Not only did Norman Wood invest all his talent and energy into Denby, he also invested his personal savings when the company was in need of capital. He was not happy when, in the seventies, the company was floated on the stock exchange. Subsequent events were to justify his unease, but he continued his involvement with the company until his retirement as Chief Executive in 1979. After that date he remained active as a consultant and director and maintained his connections with Denby until his death in 1985 at the age of seventy-six.

## THE DALES

The Dale family's connection with the Bournes began in Burslem, Stoke-on-Trent, where Robert Dale worked for Pinder, Bourne and Co. at the beginning of the nineteenth century. In 1842 Robert Dale moved to the Denby factory to take up an appointment as Works Manager. He was known as 'Colour Bob' because of his knowledge of coloured glazes and made an important contribution to the appearance of early Denby ware. A talented musician, he played the organ in the Methodist Chapel in Street Lane, a village near Denby. He died on the 4th February 1884 at the age of sixty-eight.

His musical talent was inherited by his son Christopher who was only six months old when Robert moved to Denby. Christopher joined his father at the Pottery when he was fourteen years of age and, after his training, at the

Retirement plaque presented to Norman Wood in 1979.

age of eighteen, went to the firm's London office in 1860. *The Pottery Gazette* reports that the Manager in London was one William Bourne, possibly a grandson of the first William Bourne. Christopher took over the London office in 1875. During his time in London he took a prominent part in Methodist activities being a Sunday School superintendent, organist and choirmaster and became the Honorary Principal of the Metropolitan College of Music and contributed to the Methodist hymnbook.

Christopher's son Alex joined him in the London office in 1891 and father and son worked together until Christopher's death in 1912. Alex was the obvious person to succeed his father and remained in charge until his death in 1941. Less prominent than his father in religious and musical circles, Alex was an efficient and respected manager of the Denby showroom and was joined by his son John in 1931.

John had been keen to join Denby when he left school and after a brief business course combined with some pottery training, moved from Denby to London. With Joseph and Norman Wood he helped to restore Denby's fortunes. During the Second World War, John worked at Denby after the London showroom was bombed. He had hoped to enlist after a spell in the Territorial Army but, having only one lung, failed the medical examination. Bitterly disappointed, John joined the Home Guard and also spent his nights fire-watching (i.e. an air raid precaution duty that involved guarding the factory against incendiary bombs). He and his wife Betty rented a house but he spent little time at home because of his long working hours, Home Guard and fire-watching duties. At that time Denby was making functional items such as insulators for the Post Office, rum jars for the Navy and chamber pots for prisoners, in addition to the ubiquitous foot-warmers and kitchen ware.

Left to right: John Dale, Joseph Wood and Norman Wood in the showroom, c.1951.

When the war ended, John persuaded Denby's top management to have the London showrooms repaired and re-opened. There was some resistance from the Board who felt that priority should be given to restoring the company's export market. It must have been agreed eventually that both home and export markets should have simultaneous attention. The export drive and the showrooms were equally successful. John attended all the trade fairs and helped by his wife and daughter, Susan,

made a significant impact on the British market. Susan, the fifth generation Dale, worked with her father briefly in London but left the firm in the early 1970s. John was a superb salesman who had inherited all his family's charm and flair. Immensely popular with customers and staff, he made a major contribution to Denby's post-war recovery and subsequent progress. Failing health forced him to retire on the last day of 1974, the last of the Denby Dale's.

John Dale (left) and Lionel Simons in the U.S.A., c.1969.

John and Betty Dale, c.1950.

# CHAPTER 7
# THE GLYN COLLEDGE HERITAGE

The Denby Pottery may have been owned by the Bournes and managed by the Woods and the Dales but, from the earliest days, the ware that ensured its success and for which it was famous was created, designed and decorated by Albert and Glyn Colledge, their ancestors and other skilled workers.

## THE CAULTONS

When the Pottery opened in the early nineteenth century one of its first employees was William Caulton, Glyn Colledge's great-great-grandfather, who lived in a cottage called The College across the road from the factory buildings. When William was sixty-nine his second wife, Mary, then forty-three, bore her only child John.

A remarkable man, John Caulton was a gifted inventive engineer, a musician and a devout Methodist. One of the Pottery's earliest engineers, he invented a lathe for making the screw tops on ginger beer bottles. At home he turned his inventive skills to making most of his own furniture and even a suit of clothes for his second wedding. At Street Lane Methodist Chapel he not only

superintended the Sunday School and trained the choir but, with the help of a colleague, Timothy Briggs, actually built the organ that was played by Christopher Dale. Throughout his life he kept a detailed diary and kept fit by walking throughout the Derbyshire countryside. On 25th June 1883 his diary records, 'First day at new lathe in new room – very tired! On the 21st December 1887 he wrote:

> 'Went this morning to Kings at Green Hillocks to get apparatus made for threading or tapping ginger beer bottle necks outside – stayed with Arthur King directing the operation till one o' clock, subsequently I found the machine work quite satisfactorily and when I got to Pottery it pleased Mr. Topham wonderfully.' (Mr Topham, Sarah Elizabeth Bourne's nephew, was managing the Pottery at that time).

John Caulton was married three times and had seven children. Two of the daughters by his second wife, Ann, married members of the Colledge family. Mary Anne married Charles Colledge an overlooker at Denby and Langley Mill Potteries who worked at these sites for seventy years. Ann Rebecca married George Henry Colledge, Glyn's grandfather, who was an engineer. John Caulton's son, John, worked at the Pottery as did a son-in-law, Alfred Fowke. John Caulton junior was also an organist who played at Ripley Parish Church for forty-one years.

## ALBERT COLLEDGE

George Henry and Ann Rebecca Colledge had eight children, one of whom was Albert Henry Colledge, Glyn's father and Denby's first full-time in-house designer. He was born in a terraced house in Chapel Street, Kilburn on 7th April 1891, and went to school a few miles away in Horsley. His brother, George, was a turner at Denby Pottery and, when he was thirteen, Albert went to work there as a caster. To improve his education he attended an evening class in Eastwood, five or six miles from his home. Usually he would walk to the class but sometimes stayed with his Uncle Charles who was an overlooker at Langley Mill Pottery. It was obvious from an early age that Albert had artistic talents and he was put alongside a freelance designer from Stoke-on-Trent. In his free time he put his artistic skills to work earning a few shillings as a signwriter for local shops.

When World War I broke out in 1914, Albert enlisted in the Royal Army Service Corps, serving as a driver. During the war he met his future wife, Evelyn Alice Woolley, who had come to Denby from her home in Barry, South Wales, to visit relatives. Evelyn came from a middle-class home. Her brother Charles Woolley was

Albert Colledge (seated) with Glyn in the studio, c.1948.

Albert Colledge (centre) during the First World War.

eventually knighted and made Governor and Commander in Chief of Malta and Cyprus. Albert and Evelyn's first son, Ivor, was born in 1917 and his second son, Glyn, five years later. When the Great War ended, Albert returned to Denby to resume his career as a pottery decorator.

In 1923 Albert was put in charge of the Pottery's first decorating department. It was housed in the room which now contains the factory's committee rooms and personnel office. Overlooking the main road, it contained a gas engine for spraying slip and glaze. Between that date and his retirement forty years later, Albert Colledge made an outstanding contribution to the design and decoration of Denby ware, keeping abreast of changes in style and fashion and helping other designers to bring their work to fruition. From the decoration of the early Danesby Ware in the 1920s to the design and creation of the best selling tableware in the 1950s, Albert can be said to have been one of the mainsprings of Denby's success.

During his sixty years with Denby, Albert must have decorated and designed hundreds of different shapes. Many of these are recorded in his own hand on the illustrated price lists he prepared using Gestetner stencils. Before each fair or exhibition he would draw the latest designs directly onto the stencils and the prices and descriptions would be typed alongside the drawings by one of the office staff.

Greatly respected for his skill and held in awe for his determined and somewhat autocratic manner, Albert ruled his department firmly as it grew in size and importance over the years. His decorators recall how he always checked that they had 'clean pinnies and dusters' and his son, Glyn, remembers him saying that, '...a day was not worthwhile unless there was a trial' – i.e. an experimental firing.

If a decoration was not applied correctly, Albert would wipe it out and tell the decorator to do it again. As Glyn ruefully recalls, his father applied this ruthless approach to his own son in the early days.

As seems to have been the custom at Denby, Albert continued to work long after the normal retirement age

and did not retire finally until 1963 when he was seventy-two. Glyn recalls that his father was beginning to 'wind down' in the 1960s. He lived a further nine years and died on 29th September 1972. His widow lived for another five years, until 22nd September 1977. Both were buried in the family grave in Horsley churchyard.

## GLYN COLLEDGE

Glyn Colledge, the last in the Caulton/Colledge line to work at Denby, is the one who is probably best known today. Born on 23rd July 1922 in Chapel Street, Kilburn, Glyn did not have a particularly happy childhood. He felt that he was overshadowed by his elder brother who, he thought, was spoilt by his parents and caused him trouble at school because of his high spirits. Despite his natural intelligence, Glyn disliked school. At first he attended the Marehay Junior School near Ripley and, at seven, went to Ripley's Council School. He would travel to school by bus but sometimes walked, having spent the bus fare on chocolate. On Saturday mornings he would enjoy visiting his father at work in Denby Pottery where he absorbed the atmosphere of the factory.

Glyn did not appreciate the Swanwick Hall Grammar School any more than he had the junior school and, because he was suffering from nephritis, was unable to take the School Certificate examination. In July 1938, Glyn left his hated school and joined his father at Denby Pottery as a trainee modeller at a wage of 12s6d for a forty-five hour week. Later that year his parents took him to the Burslem School of Art in Stoke-on-Trent where he had a successful interview with the principal, Gordon Forsyth, and was enrolled as a full-time student.

His student days apparently made little impact on Glyn but he still recalls the hazards of cycling to lectures over frosty cobbles and the difficulties of managing his budget. Although he was a pupil of the legendary Gordon Forsyth and attended the same college that had trained Susie Cooper, Clarice Cliff, Charlotte Rhead and Mabel Leigh, he is typically modest about his achievements there.

It may be that the impending war, followed by the war itself had an unsettling effect on the young Glyn. Some of the teachers had enlisted and those remaining seemed 'characterless' to him. In 1941 he went on to Derby's Technical College but found that no more inspiring and decided to enlist in the Royal Air Force's Air Sea Rescue Service. He served in Italy, North Africa, Malta and France as well as Great Britain. When the war ended he was able to return to Denby as a trainee designer.

At twenty-four, Glyn was becoming aware of omissions in his education and enrolled as a part-time student in the ceramics department of the Derby College of Art. Realising the value of education, he continued as a student for the next ten years and eventually became a part-time lecturer at Derby and the Ilkeston College of Further Education. In retrospect, it is surprising that Glyn felt that it was necessary for him to continue training whilst he was producing his famous Glyn Ware and other prestigious designs for Denby.

At first, as a trainee designer, Glyn worked with his father and together they created new designs for the post-war market. One of these was Flair which Glyn continued to develop whilst his father was in hospital. John Dale suggested that he should wait until his father came back but Glyn persisted so that by the time his father returned Flair was almost complete.

The Colledges would seek inspiration for their work even whilst on holiday. Glyn recalls that once, in Broadway, they saw some carved wooden animals, foxes and hounds, which inspired Albert to model similar stoneware figures when he returned to Denby. On a later occasion, while in France, Glyn designed a new shape based on a French mineral water bottle.

Gradually, he became more independent and was given the studio formerly used by Alice Teichtner from which he created Glyn Ware. To avoid the exorbitant purchase tax, each item, though decorative, was given a functional description. As a further safeguard, Glyn had to sign every piece by hand which gave them the status of studio pottery.

As the decorating department expanded from five 'girls' in 1946 to seventy by the 1960s, so Glyn's responsibilities increased. He developed new methods and techniques, in collaboration with the chemist and other technicians, which achieved the characteristic Denby look. One such technique was the 'reactive' or jewelled glaze that Glyn originated and used on Cloisonee.

One of his main functions was to ensure that the ideas of freelance designers were translated into practical reality on the factory floor. His role was to orchestrate the differing functions of designers and technicians and, to ensure that the work produced was in line with sales and management policy, he would sometimes visit designers such as Tibor Reich in their studios. In those days, Glyn recalls, in-house designers were not particularly well paid and would resent the much higher fees paid to those who were freelance. He and Albert often felt that the freelance designers were enlisted unnecessarily, but management undoubtedly considered that it was sometimes necessary to commission outside artists for specific projects.

As his father approached retirement, Glyn gradually took on more responsibility and initiated many innovations and new designs. Constantly aware of current design trends, his work developed through the New Look Fifties and Swinging Sixties, but always retained its basic artistic integrity.

Eventually his work took him to France, Poland and Portugal and he became, successively, a Director of Denby and the New Products Manager. A happy second marriage to Valerie, a colleague in the decorating department, was followed by the birth of his son, Austen, in 1977.

Unfortunately, new ownership of the Pottery in the 1980s brought about a change in design policy that was anathema to the independently-minded Glyn, and he took early retirement in 1983. The new freedom enabled him to create his own studio pottery in the garden of his idyllic country cottage. There, unhampered by commercial strictures, he was able to throw and decorate pottery that reflected his artistic ability. Not surprisingly, his pots found a ready market amongst his admirers, who are always welcomed at his home. There, they are entertained by his quiet, dry wit, quirky sense of humour and cups of tea. Conversation is interspersed by the different tunes played by his collection of clocks, all of which chime at slightly different intervals. Always willing to share his encyclopedic knowledge of Denby pottery, Glyn has been of inestimable help to the authors.

Glyn Colledge in R.A.F. uniform during the Second World War.

# CHAPTER 8
# POST-WAR RENAISSANCE
# 1946 - 1959

As Denby's workers, including Glyn Colledge, returned from the Forces, Norman Wood proceeded to implement his plans for reconstruction and to prepare for the resumption of the company's export trade.

Glyn recalls that, 'In order to get licences to re-build the factory (it was all corridors, staircases and small workshops) it was necessary to get orders for exports, these being Australia, New Zealand and Canada.'

The last major link with the Bourne family ended in 1948 when Florence Bourne-Wheeler died. Her position as Company Chairman was taken by T.G. Rawlings, a financial director. Mr. Rawlings was only to enjoy this position for a year, as he died in 1949 and Joseph Wood became Chairman. Britain's industry was gradually returning to normal under a Labour Government but, like most pottery manufacturers, Denby was impatient to resume the use of coloured glazes and, in full-page advertisements in the trade press, had been regularly promising its customers the full range of ware 'when restrictions are lifted'. During this period the company was investing heavily in such advertisements in the pottery publications to remind the trade of the factory's products and long tradition of skilled work.

The reconstruction planned during the war was reaching fruition and the company was ready to open its new showrooms at Denby in 1951 in time to join the Festival of Britain celebrations. The Government had decided to celebrate the centenary of the Great Exhibition of 1851 with a festival to demonstrate the achievements of British industry and to take the minds of the public off rationing and austerity. The Pottery submitted examples of its ware for the exhibition on London's South Bank but concentrated its energies on the fine new showrooms in rural Denby.

The trade press was highly enthusiastic about its impressive contemporary architecture. The Stoke-on-Trent firm of Wood, Goldstraw and Yorath, specialists in architecture for pottery firms, had collaborated with the designer Robert Wetmore of Cockade Limited to realise Norman Wood's vision of a light, airy showroom in the Scandinavian tradition. A curving staircase was lit from ground floor to roof level by a tall curved window of glass bricks. Terrazzo floor tiling linked long walls of acoustic tiles and glass bricks which contrasted with low walls made of Yorkshire paving stones. A discreet grey colour scheme with coned metal lighting complemented beech, mahogany and sycamore shelving on which was displayed the company's latest designs. It provided an ideal setting for the work of Glyn Colledge. Background colour was provided by Swedish artists and by John Minton, a leading

British designer of contemporary wallpaper. The showroom was furnished in the modern utility style by pieces specially designed by Robert Wetmore. No expense had been spared to use the best designers, artists and materials to complement Denby's products.

At the same time, the whole factory lay-out was being rationalised to give a single production level for all the processes – including drying, conditioning, dipping, placing, firing and warehousing. The new design was claimed to have increased production by twenty-five percent when only two-thirds of the work had been done. The whole concept was hailed as 'revolutionary' and the envy of the pottery trade. The staff's needs were catered for with a new canteen, cloakrooms and sanitary facilities. The tiles in the cloakrooms were decorated with scenes of pottery life drawn by Glyn Colledge.

By this time Norman Wood and John Dale were Works Director and Sales Director respectively, and the firm had over four hundred employees. Traditional wares were phased out and dinner ware was introduced for the first time together with more sophisticated tablewares. Albert Colledge, as chief designer, is credited with introducing the first dinner ware at Denby. Glyn records that eventually:

> 'The same shapes were produced with several glaze finishes and decorations. The influence of the U.S. agent was now beginning to dictate patterns and co-incided with a lot of time wasted by market testing which tended to take the heart out of the original conception.'

Contemporary architecture at the Denby showroom, 1951.

The new showroom, 1951.

The 1951 Festival was followed in 1953 by another spectacular event, the Coronation of Elizabeth II, an occasion celebrated with commemorative ware in the Denby tradition. Albert and Glyn Colledge's designs were selling even more successfully with the lifting of restrictions on the manufacture of decorative pottery in 1952 and the factory was free to produce new lines in coloured ware.

In 1956 one of Denby's most successful lines was Greenwheat Tableware designed by Albert Colledge, then aged sixty-five. His son, Glyn, records that:

> 'Two things led to its success, firstly the Bank Clerk's wife could buy one piece a month – not so Wedgwood and Doulton etc. and secondly, the sales manager of the time, John Dale, had the vision to compare the above two companies' prices and ensure that Denby's prices were competitive. This pricing put Denby on the top shelf with the public and the buyers. This shape range ran for almost thirty years.'

In keeping with his policy of recruiting the leading designers in their field, Norman Wood commissioned Tibor Reich and Kenneth Clark to develop specific projects. Tibor's unique style enlivened the Company's giftware range and Kenneth's classic shapes brought new prestige to its cookware.

## TIBOR REICH

Tibor Reich, an extraordinary textile virtuoso with a flair for design and colour, was one of Denby's most successful and remarkable designers of the 1950s. Where Alice Teichtner had brought the influence of Austrian culture and the Vienna Werkstadt to rural Denby, Tibor's work reflected his Hungarian background and the philosophy of the Weimar Bauhaus, which, whilst espousing a return to traditional form also developed prototypes for industrial production.

Born in Budapest to a weaving family in 1916, Tibor's formal education was at the Textile School of Vienna and the University and College of Art in Leeds but he learned much about colour and design in the countryside of his native Hungary and amongst the dyes and fabrics of his father's workshop where the ribbons for peasant costumes were made. Tibor spent five years at Leeds, three on the study of textile technology and design and two on scientific research. A contemporary journalist records that he had:

> '...almost a childlike curiosity about both simple and complicated things, a love of experiment and nature, a fascination for and a magic skill in dealing with colours and...a large amount of idealism.'

Indeed, one of his maxims was 'Nature designs best'.

After graduating with distinction at Leeds in 1942, Tibor's work attracted the attention of the aristocratic fashion designer Captain Edward Molyneux who used a 'Leopard Tweed' designed by Tibor for his 1945 United States export collection. The interest of the House of Molyneux brought Tibor's work to a wider audience and helped him to build up a textile business of international proportions, based in Stratford-upon-Avon where he lived with his wife Freda, a former concert pianist.

Tibor's success in textiles stemmed from innovative designs, an inspired feel for colour, and his development of ingenious techniques, such as Fotexur that transformed

Tibor and Freda Reich, mid-1950s.

photographs of natural textures into fabric designs. As he developed his textile materials to include curtains, tapestries, upholstery and carpets, Tibor displayed his products in complete interior settings including furniture and ceramics. He believed that black and white pottery would be not only a focal point in a room but also an excellent foil for the bright, bold colours and patterns of contemporary furnishing. None of the products currently on the market were satisfactory for Tibor's exacting requirements. Typically, he set up a small pottery kiln near Stratford-upon-Avon and employed a studio potter to make such pots to his design.

Although successful in producing prototypes, and small-scale production, the Pottery did not have the capacity to meet the demands of Tibor's growing organisation. He therefore approached Denby in 1953 with the proposal that they should produce his original pottery. Norman Wood recognised his talent and readily agreed, enrolling Tibor as a consultant and merging the small Tigo pottery company with Denby. The flamboyant Reichs are said to have 'fluttered a few feathers' when they visited the factory, and the Tigo Ware, as it was known, made a distinctive contribution to Denby pottery. Alongside Glyn Colledge's elegant Cheviot vases the two typically fifties designs made a spectacular display when they were first exhibited at the London Tea Centre in 1956.

Tibor's association with Denby was comparatively brief. Ceramic ware was a small but important facet of the wide Tibor spectrum. Nevertheless, one of his vases was illustrated as the epitomè of good contemporary design alongside the legendary Wedgwood Portland Vase, on the cover of *Seven Thousand Years of Pottery and Porcelain* by Max Wykes-Joyce.

Whilst he was working with Denby, Tibor was also designing his own experimental house in which he lived near Stratford-upon-Avon. Although not an architect, Tibor introduced many innovative features that were later adopted by the building industry.

He went on to design more fabrics and tapestries for castles, palaces, cathedrals, numbers 10 and 11 Downing Street, and even Concorde. Tibor Reich is recognised to have made a significant contribution to twentieth-century design. The *Design* magazine describes him as '...one of the few woven textile designers who have contributed to the language of weaving.' In 1973 Tibor was awarded the Textile Institute's Design Medal for 'his unique contribution to the design of furnishing fabrics.'

As an adopted son of Stratford-upon-Avon he became fully involved in the tourist industry surrounding William Shakespeare. He designed all the fabrics for the Shakespeare Memorial Theatre, and created many posters, tapestries and souvenir materials. He went on to design carpets and fabrics for the Shakespeare Centre that was opened to commemorate the 400th anniversary of Shakespeare's birth. Tibor even put his hobby of collecting model cars to the service of the town by opening a Model Car Museum to display the 6000 items.

With his multi-faceted talents and his capacity for solving all types of design problems, Tibor Reich can truly be described as a 'Renaissance man'.

## KENNETH CLARK

Kenneth Clark became associated with Denby in 1956. His work had the classic style that Norman Wood admired and contributed to Denby's continuing success.

Kenneth Clark is '...one of those names which constantly crop up whenever mention is made of industrial design', according to *The Pottery Gazette* of October 1960. Listed by the Council of Industrial Design, he must have seemed an obvious choice when Denby decided to up-date its oven-to-tableware in the 1950s. Although his association with the Pottery was comparatively brief, his impact was a significant milestone in the history of Denby design.

When he left the Navy after World War II, Kenneth

An exhibition display of Denby pottery at the London Tea Centre, 1956.

Kenneth Clark, 1956.

Clark trained as a painter at the Slade School of Fine Art. In the late 1940s very few painters were able to make even a modest living from their work so Kenneth started teaching part-time and studying pottery. The prospect of making a living as a potter was good as the demand at the time was considerable. While working at Lakes Cornish Pottery in Truro during a vacation, he met Ronald Copeland of Copeland-Spode who invited him to visit the factory should he be visiting Stoke-on-Trent. When an opportunity did arise he visited the Copeland factory and gained permission to work there, unpaid, in order to gain industrial experience. This greatly stimulated his ambition to become both an industrial designer as well as a maker of individual and industrial ceramics.

In the early 1950s he started his own pottery in central London and was soon joined by his talented wife Ann who had recently been a student at the Central School of Art and Design where he was a part-time tutor. Using his Stoke experience, Kenneth designed and produced a range of industrial ceramics which he endeavoured to have manufactured under contract in Stoke. Whilst showing the designs to Roy Midwinter of Midwinter Pottery, Roy offered to market them for him should he come and set up a manufacturing business in Stoke. As he felt he was more a 'hands-on' person, rather than one to manage a factory, he reluctantly declined the generous offer.

In their studio pottery in London, Kenneth and Ann designed and produced a remarkable variety of ceramics for restaurants, cinemas and other public buildings. As a result of his experience, he used many industrial techniques, though the emphasis was always on hand-decoration. These two aspects of his work were a great help and inspiration when he was asked to design for Denby which had a strong tradition of industrial making and hand-decorating.

## END OF DECADE

As Denby's 150th anniversary approached, the company's reputation was being enhanced at home and abroad. In the year of the anniversary, 1959, a new showroom was opened in Thavies Inn House, Holborn Circus, London, again in the contemporary style pioneered at Denby. To mark the anniversary, Albert Colledge designed a special mug, but the celebrations were not as flamboyant as those in 1909. They were, nevertheless, duly reported in the trade and local press. The celebrations were attended by Charles and Hugh Chittenden, two members of the Bourne dynasty who had attended the centenary occasion in 1909. Speaking at the 1959 event, Norman Wood referred to recent improvements in the company which, '...had put one or two more stitches into the Denby tapestry which (would) both extend and enrich its pattern.'

In the same year, Denby took over the failing Langley Mill Pottery for a reported £25,000, to prevent it falling into the hands of competitors. A management team led by Fred Cooper and including Glyn Colledge was sent to revive the declining factory. Fred Cooper came from the Royal Navy to become a trainee manager. He was eventually promoted to Works Manager at Denby and Managing Director at Langley. According to staff who worked there, 'Denby was the brand leader and at first Langley was something of a poor relation.' The Denby team eventually won the goodwill of the Langley staff and together they built up the factory into an up-to-date, viable unit that complemented the main Denby headquarters. At first, each company continued to trade separately under its original name.

At the time of the take-over, Langley Mill Pottery was managed by the three Mitchell brothers, Ron, Harry and Frank. Ron was eventually made a director of the Denby company and, together with Glyn, developed screen printing techniques and new tableware designs.

Fred Cooper.

# THE NEW LOOK

After the war there was a period of austerity when food and clothes were rationed and when pottery was deprived of colour. Denby's brown utility ware was promoted as, 'The Pot that keeps food hot'. In a series of advertisements, customers were reminded that successful cooks needed Denby pots in order to make a tempting cauliflower cheese, an Irish stew or a chicken casserole. It was not, however, until the mid-1950s that Denby produced a series of oven-to-tableware that was contemporary in style. Eventually, when restrictions were relaxed, Donald Gilbert's Cottage Blue and Manor Green were re-issued and a new colourway introduced in 1953.

**Homestead Brown,** *on the same shapes, was glazed in a rich brown with a contrasting lavender-blue interior.*

The direction of post-war production was profoundly influenced by the introduction of new machines and techniques for plate making. The firm began to specialise in the manufacture of dinner and tableware. Traditional design still predominated but, from the time that Albert Colledge designed the first dinner ware in 1947/8, significant changes in style and emphasis were to occur. A first-hand report by his son Glyn records that:

> 'Plates were developed by the need to change from kitchen ware to dinner ware; a man from Stoke named Albert Gibson was enticed to work at Denby, his know-how of flatware and its foibles was seized upon and at last Denby could make stoneware plates that 'sprang' off the mould and kept shape. Plate making machines were hired by the year from Stoke engineering firms, ovals were hand jollied, and of course T.V. snack trays (U.S. influence) and oblong platters were cast from stock moulds. So you see, flatware was designed by necessity and ability; years went by before it was modified to a flatter edge (three-fifths of an inch at the most) and it was the late sixties before a rim plate evolved. The first dinner ware shape for hollow ware was designed by my father, Albert Colledge.

**Flair** *dinner ware, produced in 1947, was the combined work of Albert and Glyn Colledge. Red, brown and green cockerels sketched in free-brush strokes, strode purposefully across white plates. Each size or shape of pot displayed the bird in a different activity, pecking for corn or chasing a rabbit. On the oval dishes, hounds chased a fox, 'all entertaining', to quote Glyn. Flair was made for the export market and consequently only a few cockerels were liberated in the Denby area.*

**Peasant Ware,** *introduced in 1954, was a transitional design which, whilst retaining the traditional characteristics of Denby pottery, also acknowledged modern influences. It created an impression of rural simplicity with a rustic style which bore comparison with the French faience made at Quimper in Brittany. The gently curving shapes and looped handles were glazed in a soft grey with an interior rinsed in pale-pink. The abstract, hand-painted scroll and leaf pattern in grey and yellow, was contemporary in style.*

Peasant Ware shapes were hand-decorated in a variety of ways: simply glazed, hand-painted, tube-lined or banded. The banding was done by Mrs. Potts from Stoke-on-Trent and Florence Ashmore, who were specialists in this technique. It is to Albert Colledge's credit that these very different decorative effects could be applied so successfully to his basic shapes.

**Dovedale,** *glazed in the modern idiom with a dark-grey exterior and a bright yellow interior, was issued the year after Peasant Ware.*

**Suburban** *was decorated with a peppered stone and iron glaze.*

**Dream** *was glazed in white, with grey interiors and a hand-painted moon and stars.*

**Twilight,** *on a grey ground, was banded and decorated with tube-lined spots.*

**Pride,** *in mid-blue, was banded in blue, with a scrolled design by Albert Colledge.*

**Spring,** *by Glyn, was white-glazed with grey interiors, grey banding and stylised leaf and bud.*

Lithographs were introduced but, although pretty, were a poor substitute for hand-decorated ware.

**Charm,** *with its stylised rose was the first transfer print, made in Stoke-on-Trent, to be used by Denby. It was produced solely for export.*

**Beauty** *bore a similar, but single, long-stemmed rose.*

The new hand-painted tableware issued in 1956, was an immediate success with the public. Greenwheat by Albert Colledge was different in style from ware currently being sold by other potteries. The confidence which Denby had in the new design and the high regard in which they held its designer, was demonstrated by a high-profile advertising campaign and by the addition of Albert Colledge's signature to the ware.

**Greenwheat,** *with the same white ground as that used for Flair but with contrasting dark-green interior and handles, displayed a fresh, hand-painted spray of wheat-ears and leaves that was appropriate in most homes. Audrey Jackson, who had previously decorated Glyn Ware, painted the first Greenwheat. The minimalist design was inspired by the decorative brush-strokes of early Japanese potters whose influence was reflected in the work of British studio potters such as Bernard Leach. The design of Greenwheat was a commercial development of this tradition. Its universal appeal, combined with the strength and durability of the pottery, ensured that it remained one of Denby's best selling lines for over twenty years. Again, Albert Colledge had successfully combined the traditional with the modern.*

**Harvest,** *decorated in brown, was eventually issued especially for the United States and Canadian markets.*

Norman Wood and John Dale, always conscious of the latest design trends, decided that some of Donald Gilbert's earlier shapes should be presented in bold, contemporary colours.

**Eclipse**, *marketed at the same time as Greenwheat, was based on Donald Gilbert's 1939 shapes and glazed in a contemporary colourway. Its shiny black glaze with contrasting white interior and lids, was complementary to decorative ware that was currently being produced by the art department. In early sets, some plates were black and some were white, but as the black plates scratched easily, later plates were always white.*

Fred Cooper, the manager of Langley Pottery, masterminded a tableware series for Denby which was designed specifically for T. Eaton and Company Limited of Canada. The range, which was a great success in North America, had been influenced by the work of an American designer, Russell Wright.

**Gala** *tableware was not made of Denby clay. It consisted of a white body glazed in rich, bright colours – purple, green, turquoise-blue, yellow, maroon and grey. The handles were looped, the shapes outrageous, the colours vivid.*

Tableware designed in 1956, by Tibor Reich, a freelance designer, was typical of the 1950s in style, colour and decoration.

**Tigo Ware**, *in contrasting black and white, is described in the section on Decorative Ware.*

**Marguerita**, *glazed in white, with hollows and occasional lids in grey, was decorated with a simple flower sketched in black lines and highlighted by a yellow centre.*

A range of gift ware and table accessories was specifically designed for the modern home currently being transformed by a profusion of contemporary designs on carpets, curtains and crockery. Intended to supplement other Denby wares it was part of a successful policy of mix-and-match.

Glyn reports that:

'Gift ware lines, bowls, planters, jugs etc. were all hand-thrown and turned and could be changed relatively easily to show a different effect to please the 'sales reps' and enhance the trade fairs. Usually these lines were changed when interest faded – some lasted only one year – others, like Glynbourne, for about eight years. The important thing was that each new offer employed a new technique, even though all ware was once-fired from clay, and employed etching, banding, texture spraying, dry brush techniques etc. The same system operated for dinner ware and gift ware at Langley Pottery after the take-over in 1959.'

**Boutique** *gift ware was organised in 1956 by Norman Wood to complement Eclipse tableware and the contemporary decorative designs of Glyn Colledge and Tibor Reich. It included Glyn's simple modern shapes in bold and subtle colours to contrast with the black and white Tigo Ware designed by Tibor.*

With the success of Greenwheat tableware the time

Barbara Middleton, a post-war paintress at the Pottery.

was appropriate for a new assessment to be made of oven-to-tableware. Denby Pottery increasingly reflected the influence of a changing society with its more informal life-style and responded to ideas emerging from the London Design Centre which was sponsored by the Council of Industrial Design.

These factors were to influence Norman Wood when he invited Kenneth Clark, with his established reputation for the design of contemporary-styled ceramics, to create a modern image for Denby oven-to-tableware.

## KENNETH CLARK

On being commissioned by Denby in 1956 to design a new oven-to-tableware range, Kenneth Clark aimed to refine the traditional shapes and to exploit the natural qualities of Denby clay. In the first instance he would throw a prototype and would then sit with the paintresses to demonstrate and advise on the appropriate decorating techniques.

**Gourmet (first version)** *was a classic design for the sophisticated table. Introduced in 1957 it was stylish and beautifully proportioned, reflecting the precision with which it had been designed. The shapes were carefully honed as he pursued his aim of perfect form combined with fitness for purpose. His detailed drawings formed a blueprint for the range. Because all Denby shapes were hand-thrown there was a tendency towards natural curving lines. Kenneth Clark wanted the upper part of Gourmet to have a straight profile which would contrast with the roundness below. This was difficult for the throwers to achieve and over the years an overall rotundity was allowed to develop, thus weakening the strength of the original design.*

Kenneth Clark's,

'...initial idea was not to cover the body but actually make the natural colour of the fired body a feature of the design. The decoration was a series of sgraffito lines of varying widths, scratched through a semi-matt white glaze which contrasted with the half-tone colour of the body. Each piece was finished off with a brushed black line round the top rim.

This concept was based on a well-tried and proven tradition on which many decorative designs of the past were based; a successful balance and relationship of black, white and half-tone qualities or colours.'

# DECORATIVE WARE

Denby was able to take centre stage with its decorative pottery because of the calibre of its in-house designers Albert and Glyn Colledge, two freelance designers, Tibor Reich and Kenneth Clark, and the skill and commitment of its craftspeople.

The talent of Glyn Colledge played a major part in the revitalisation of Denby's art department in the post-war period and throughout the 1950s. His design skills, together with the expertise of his father, consolidated the firm's post-war position as the country's leading manufacturer of decorative stoneware. The Colledges were responsible for the administration of the decorating department although the team approach prevailed. There was a constant exchange of ideas between the Colledges, chemists, throwers and decorators, all of whom were essential to Denby's success.

The normal practice was for Albert and Glyn to create at least one trial piece each and every day. The results of these trials and experiments were the high-spot of the day and 'the chemistry' of the designs, both in the literal and the metaphorical sense of the word, were moments of revelation.

# ALBERT COLLEDGE

In the post-war period Albert Colledge's main efforts were directed towards the production of dinner and tableware. He did, however, devise several decorative series in the late 1940s and early 1950s, most of which were adapted from Denby's nineteenth-century relief moulded hunting jugs. Because of Government restrictions the ware could only be produced for export. Design tended to be derivative and original work was at a premium.

**Tally Ho** *was the first decorative ware produced by Denby after the war. Searching for new ideas, Albert found some of the original 'sprigs' and, consequently, in 1946, horses and hounds again galloped around tankards and jugs in chase of a fox. To up-date the series, handles and rims were hand-gilded and the animals, hand-painted in natural colours, were set against a pale-green ground. They are rare today as most were sent to North America and Canada.*

**Antique,** *displaying lively hunting scenes on an antique-finished cream ground, was magnificent with richly gilded handles and lips.*

**Festive** *was based on a group of revellers in celebratory mood, seated around a table with raised tankards. It was gilded and glazed in beige with an antique finish and contrasting dark brown interiors.*

**Tally Ho**, c.1946.

**Gay Border,** *an Albert Colledge design of 1948, was similar in style to the work he had produced pre-war. It comprised a series of ten green vases, jugs and bowls, some with twisted handles, each with a bunch of raised, hand-painted flowers.*

# GLYN COLLEDGE

During this period the real creativity and artistic generation of Danesby Ware came from a series of highly individual designs by Glyn Colledge. His work was varied in style and in technique because of his understanding of glazes and his knowledge of pottery production. It was unified by his sense of form and colour and by his natural flair and artistic integrity.

An independent reporter from *The Pottery and Glass Record* of 1949 records that:

'The artistic apex at Denby is the studio pottery installed within the works. This is the domain of Glynn...a young studio potter...now back at the wheel throwing pots of considerable beauty and appeal. The majority of the 'Glynn' pots are marketed as individual pieces but some of his designs are set aside as prototypes for quantity production in the factory...Prices for Glynn's pots are rightly high but this has proved to be no bar to success.'

Although many contemporary sources refer to Glynn Ware (two n's), Glyn's preference is for Glyn Ware and his version has been used throughout this book.

**Original Glyn Ware,** *although experimental in nature, exhibited the original style that was to be the hallmark of Glyn Colledge's future work. A horse, a deer, a lion, a sea-horse, and a fish were tube-lined and occasionally hand-painted. Unfortunately, the tube-lining did not always adhere to the pot and technical problems led to some crazing of the glaze. The pieces are attractive in their own right but doubly so because of their rarity and the fact that they were the precursor of Glyn Ware one of the most successful of the Danesby Ware series. Entirely his own work, they were signed 'Glynn' in green and bore a black backstamp, 'Made in England'. Glyn himself cannot explain why his signature on the Original Glyn Ware includes an extra letter 'n'.*

**Glyndebourne** *was created by Glyn between 1948 and 1950. Denby is reported to have been one giant studio pottery and, at this period, it was centred around the work of Glyn Colledge. A series of original, traditionally hand-thrown shapes with* *horizontally-ribbed surfaces was glazed in merging soft pastel shades and decorated with green, grey, and deep pink impressionistic leaves and flowers, hand-painted in the Chinese style. These pieces are amongst the most rare ever created by Glyn Colledge and confirm his status as a true studio potter.*

**Glyn Ware** *was the best known of all Glyn's designs combining quality with popular appeal. The diversity of the hand-painting was unified by the coherence of the shapes. Glyn's own highly individual style was immediately recognisable. Every piece was assessed and approved by him before it received his signature, 'Glyn', written, often illegibly, with his left hand.*

*An infinite variety of leaves in soft vibrant colours trailed across gently curving shapes. The integrity of the natural shapes and organic designs ensured that its appeal would last beyond the generation for which it was first created. Indeed, it is appreciated as much today as it was when Glyn designed it in 1950.*

*Initially no flowers were allowed because Glyn wished to avoid the prettiness associated with many of the floral transfer prints emanating from Stoke-on-Trent and which he considered unsuitable for Denby stoneware. However, a few eventually 'snook in' and pots decorated with flowers or both leaves and flowers may be found. Occasionally pieces featured hunting scenes, coaching inns, and nursery rhymes, such as Bo Peep with her sheep.*

Glyn's love of colour was stimulated by the brilliant colours of Italian majolica but his main influence has been that of Persian pottery. Today, he still seeks inspiration from his battered but treasured copy of *A Guide to the Islamic Pottery of the Near East* by P.L. Hobson, published in 1932.

It was the soft and subtle blending and merging of many harmonious colours on one pot that characterised Glyn Ware. Glyn recalls that one of his tutors from the Derby College of Art, Stanley Crocker, later to become Principal of Taunton College of Art, introduced him to the idea of adding glycerine to the colours to make them flow.

Jugs were balanced by boldly-curved handles, some uniquely decorated. One day Glyn and his father returned from a trip to London, having bought a pastry roller. Glyn proceeded to use it, not in the kitchen, but in the Denby decorating workshop where he cut out strips of clay which were then rolled to produce the effect of tiny leaves and buds. These were then applied to the handles of his pots. A simple idea, a simple tool and Glyn Ware jugs acquired their distinctive, floral handles.

Glyn himself chose and experimented with small quantities of colour using a palette knife on glass. Once he was satisfied, he asked the chemist to reproduce the exact proportions for large-scale production. The colour combinations, the variety, the richness and the subtlety made Glyn Ware a design for all seasons.

Although Glyn had drawn the shapes to scale, he painted his original designs directly onto the pot which were then copied by a member of his decorating team. This group of eight young women, always known as 'the girls'

whatever their age, had originally been employed by Albert Colledge. Glyn retrained them in the basic brush strokes he required for Glyn Ware. Each girl marked her work with a coloured dot. This did not confirm, categorically, the paintress's identity because when a girl left, the replacement took over her predecessor's mark.

Audrey Jackson used a **Black** spot; Joan Corbett a **Yellow**; Gwenda Allsop a **Blue**; Olga Gration an **Orange**; Joan Baker a **Blue**; and Veronica Wilson a **Brown**. Glyn never marked his work, so pieces without a spot are almost certainly hand-painted by him.

Glyn had his own special team of craftsmen: Jim Seal 'the best' thrower who shaped his pots; Albert Blancheon, 'the best' turner, who refined them; and Fred Statham, 'the best' figureman, who made and applied all the handles and lips. The translation of his colours onto a commercial scale was effected by Douglas Stone, a 'brilliant chemist'. Glyn generously acknowledges the invaluable contribution made by them and his 'girls'. Indeed it was their skills, together with his expertise and artistic flair, which created the curving shapes and the subtle luminous colours of Glyn Ware.

## CONTEMPORARY INFLUENCES

As the decade progressed traditional influences waned and, increasingly, designs reflected the contemporary style of the 1950s.

**New Glyn Ware** *was a later, more controlled and restricted version of Glyn Ware. Curving bowls and dishes made from white earthenware displayed leaf decorations which had almost as much in common with Glyn's fabric-influenced designs as with his earlier Glyn Ware.*

**New Glyn Ware**, mid-1950s.

# GLYN AND ALBERT COLLEDGE

Glyn and his father produced a succession of decorative designs in the mid-1950s, the most commercially successful of which was Ferndale on which they collaborated.

**Ferndale** *was based on shapes by Albert Colledge. Glazed in pale-green with a satin finish they were decorated by Glyn with fine white tube-lined scrolls.*

**Celadon** *was the work of Albert Colledge in which a white abstract or stylised leaf pattern was tube-lined under the glaze on pale-green curving shapes. It was a subtle design with a glaze and simplicity reminiscent of early Chinese ware.*

**Hazelwood**, *designed by Glyn, had a rustic appearance in which thickly hand-painted 'blackberry' stripes were set vertically onto vases, jugs and asymmetric bowls, the latter displaying a free-hand, abstract pattern.*

**Crystalline**, *also the work of Glyn Colledge, was covered in a speckled, off-white glaze and then decorated with a small spray of three stylised leaves in natural colours. Handled vases and jugs were flattened slightly and bowls were asymmetrical.*

**Cretonne**, *another Glyn design, was lightly textured, mottled, flecked and matt-glazed in a creamy-brown, ochre or grey-blue. The overall pattern of spiky leaves and flowers set on vertical stems would also have been appropriate if printed on textiles.*

**Tapestry** *displayed a bold leaf design very similar to those appearing on curtain material in the 1950s. It was applied, in autumn colours, to a surface simulating fabric.*

Decorative designs proliferated, some making a brief appearance, some undocumented.

> 'Pottery is a live art. Throughout history it has reflected the life of its time; the standards of living, the level of culture, – even the political scene can be interpreted through the pottery of the past.'

This statement by Denby in the mid-1950s was backed by two major series which epitomised the period – Tigo Ware by Tibor Reich and Cheviot Ware by Glyn Colledge. A third basic series in the same genre was unattributed.

**Brightstone** *was devised in the modern idiom to 'mix and match'. Strong shapes some asymmetric were highly-glazed in black, lime-green, sea-green, and pale, moonstone-grey.*

# TIBOR REICH

Tibor, a freelance designer, worked for Denby briefly during the mid-1950s. Working on specially imported white clay he produced original designs of beauty, style and balance.

**Tigo Ware** *was designed by Tibor Reich to complement and enhance contemporary homes. It had a unique style that was essentially sophisticated, highlighted by flashes of gentle humour. The beauty and originality of the ware ensured from the outset that the functional aspect of the pottery was*

**Hazelwood**, mid-1950s.

*outweighed by its aesthetic impact. Tibor Reich did not favour extremes, preferring fundamental and practical forms that were the essence of classic design. He created organic shapes, some symmetrical, some with a judicially balanced asymmetry that transformed a pot into an object of beauty.*

*The first impression created by the Tigo coffee pot was that of a beautiful object rather than an item of tableware. The handle and spout, by their shape, angle and relationship to the body of the pot, were so much part of a balanced whole that the mind did not immediately register its function. The expressive curving lines were enhanced by the tactile quality of the black, lightly textured, matt-glazed surface. This was scratched using the sgraffito technique, to expose the white earthenware body beneath, before being sealed by a transparent glaze. The functional pots were usually decorated with vertical, sgraffitoed lines which echoed and emphasised their natural shapes.*

*Two condiment sets were made, one in the classic style with vertical lines and the other in humorous vein, in which an asymmetric salt and pepper pot embrace the centrally placed mustard pot. Obviously decorative, with sgraffito clown faces, they were actually very practical to use.*

*Tibor Reich's wall plaques were beautifully executed by the decorators at Denby. Using a fine graduation of flowing lines they created the austere, mystical figures of 'The Three Sisters' and 'The Knight'. On the 'Black Moon' plate the colours were reversed, on another a mythical Wuzu bird echoed the curve of the plate.*

Tibor Reich wall plaques, mid-1950s.

Fotexur tray, mid-1950s.

Cheviot ware, mid-1950s.

The influence of Picasso was evident in the free-standing Madar bird and in the large curving vases which were decorated to portray women. One named 'Florence', was created as a tribute to his wife who was pregnant at the time. The finely detailed figures were integrated into the shape of the pots. The humorous quality of the rotund vases was apparent in the novelty of the design but the Spanish lady, 'Espanola', with mantilla, decolletage and winking eye, conveyed a broader sense of humour.

Glyn Colledge liaised with Tibor Reich throughout the project and organised its production at Denby. It was he who copied the original drawing onto the plate to provide a master copy. The 'girls' who decorated the ware, found it very demanding as the black glaze turned into dusty grit when they scratched the designs. They then had to blow the dust away when they had completed a line so that they could see where the next line should go. It was very dirty work.

Following the success of the stark, black and white Tigo Ware, the range was extended and brilliantly-coloured glazes were applied to organic shapes. A naturally shaped 'Paprika' dish and a small, three-pointed tray were glazed in red, a long dish was coloured yellow and a large fish-shaped hors d'oeuvres tray, deep pink.

**Fotexur**, the invention of Tibor Reich, was applied to Denby pottery as well as to textiles. Detailed photographic segments of natural objects were organised into repeating patterns. These designs based on straw, tree-bark, and stones were screen-printed onto a selection of his vases, trays and dishes. Many appeared in black and white, others in natural earth colours.

## GLYN COLLEDGE

Glyn had assimilated the atmosphere and ideas generated in the mid-1950s. His interpretation of these was reflected in a series of contemporary styled decorative vases which were exhibited simultaneously with Tibor Reich's Tigo Ware.

**Cheviot** was quite different from any of Glyn's previous work. It reflected his awareness of the latest design trends and demonstrated his flexibility. The tall, slender, tapering vases were beautifully proportioned. Extremely difficult to execute, they were thrown by Jim Seal and finished by Albert Blancheon. The elegant silhouettes were judged to be beautiful enough to be presented in a white matt glaze so that nothing would detract from their classic shapes. One vase was waisted and others were variations on a theme, the source of which was a Perrier Water bottle which Glyn had first noticed on a cafe table whilst on holiday in France.

The contemporary bowls Glyn designed were thrown and turned in the usual way and then Fred Statham, Glyn's figureman, cut out either elliptical shapes or a pointed ellipse from the upper rim. This created the modern asymmetrical look. Simple moulded trays were included in the range and all were signed by Glyn himself.

Glyn, with his love of colour and decoration, could not resist embellishing Cheviot. He created one version with a matt finish, in black, dark-grey or khaki, which was covered in finely-drawn, abstract sgraffito, often including crystals, stars or simple, stylised leaves. A second highly-coloured version was glazed in yellow, blue or lilac, with black tube-lining, or in red or green, with white tube-lining. Some patterns were geometric, some herring-bone and others were organic.

## KENNETH CLARK

Three series of contemporary styled vases were designed by Kenneth Clark in 1956. It was unfortunate that they were only marketed on a limited scale.

**Cotswold** (first version) echoed the shapes of his original Gourmet oven-to-tableware with identical white glaze and sgraffito decoration which exposed the soft tone of the clay beneath.

**Asphodel**'s bold, sculptural, asymmetrical shapes were each glazed in two natural earth colours. The soft line effected by the two merging glazes emphasised the curving lines of each pot. One unusual four-legged vase was based on a Gypsy kettle.

**Single Flower Holders** with a gently curving silhouette, were glazed to match Asphodel, or in a single, vivid contemporary colour.

A later series designed towards the end of the decade was not marketed until 1960.

**Classic Ware** was created in grey with restrained vertical white stripes and marketed in 1960.

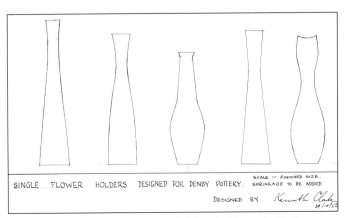
SINGLE FLOWER HOLDERS DESIGNED FOR DENBY POTTERY. SCALE :- FINISHED SIZE. SHRINKAGE TO BE ADDED.
DESIGNED BY Kenneth Clark

Working drawings for single flower-holders, by Kenneth Clark.

# GLYN AND ALBERT COLLEDGE

In the same year, Glyn and Albert Colledge again collaborated to produce a range of contemporary styled gift ware.

**Cloisonne** *was issued in 1957 on shapes designed by Albert Colledge with decoration by Glyn. The matt grey surface was highlighted by thick jewel-like colours in red, green, blue, yellow, and white, applied mainly to flatware because of the tendency of the glazes to run. Cloisonne was decorated with abstract designs and stylised domestic items including bottles, fruits, and vegetables in a manner typical of the 1950s. Colourful cockerels, regally displaying their plumage, were unlikely stablemates for the Three Kings which also decorated the ware. The birds were the direct descendants of the Flair cockerels which Glyn had drawn for his father's shapes ten years previously.*

The decade ended with two successful designs one by Glyn and one by Albert Colledge.

**Freestone** *was a typical Glyn, 'fabric-inspired' series. Matt-glazed in grey, with a base ringed in brown, it displayed a spiky plant on a cream panel.*

**Burlington** *unlike Albert's usual work was in the contemporary style. It was glazed in matt black and decorated with white, vertical broken lines. It was later issued in turquoise-blue and in multi-coloured pastels. Very rarely the shapes were decorated with vertical bands of geometric patterns. It was advertised in The Pottery Gazette of 1959 as a*

> 'new design of high originality and charm for the home of the moment; ware which blends rural simplicity with the sophistication of fine line and proportion'.

Albert Colledge was then sixty-eight years of age and had worked for Denby for fifty-five years.

Albert and Glyn Colledge remained 'constant as the Northern star' in the Denby firmament, whilst freelance designers appeared like meteors illuminating the scene with flashes of brilliance.

**Cloisonne**, c.1957.

**Asphodel**, mid-1950s.

# CHAPTER 9

# FAR HORIZONS
## 1960 - 1975

Gill Pemberton working on a **Chevron** coffee pot in the early 1960s.

## GILL PEMBERTON

At the end of every course at the Royal College of Art, manufacturers were invited to see an exhibition of the students' work with a view to employing them as designers or graphic artists. In 1960, when John Dale visited the Royal College, he was so impressed by the catering ware designs of one student that he persuaded Norman Wood to travel from Denby to view the exhibition. The student was Gill Pemberton and Norman Wood was equally enthusiastic about her designs. He immediately asked her to visit Denby to discuss working there. Gill, who had by then completed four years at the Birmingham School of Art and three at the R.C.A., knew her work was good and was in no hurry to accept the first offer of employment. British Rail was interested in her designs for catering ware and she had an offer of work at the Hornsea Pottery.

However, Gill felt 'that there seemed to be a gap she could fill...' at Denby and accepted Norman Wood's offer of employment. When she reported for work she was disappointed to find that she was expected to work at the old-fashioned Langley Pottery which had just been taken over by Denby. Working three days a week for a salary of £400 per annum, Gill spent the first nine months on what she describes as 'run of the mill' work and was almost ready to leave. Eventually, however, she became involved in creating her own demanding designs and developed a great respect for the skilled workers at Denby and Langley.

Consequently, she stayed with Denby for twenty-one years. During that time she had three children, returning to work after the birth of each.

At the time, Albert and Glyn Colledge were in charge of the decorating department, but, at first, Gill did not work closely with them. Her modus operandi was to work alongside the throwers and modellers, designing directly onto the clay and rarely making drawings other than the occasional sketch on a cigarette packet or on the nearest wall.

In 1961, Gill married a silversmith, Neil Harding, who won a travelling scholarship for a study tour of Scandinavia. With him, in 1962, she visited Denmark, Sweden, Finland and, finally, Russia. On her return, Gill designed Arabesque tableware and much of the publicity material associated with this range. It has been suggested that Gill was also inspired to design Chevron whilst in Denmark, but Gill says the choice of glaze had been completed before that visit. It is necessary for designers to be at least two years ahead of public taste and Gill was anticipating the distinctive sixties style even before she left the R.C.A.

## HOME AND ABROAD

Chevron tableware was an outstanding success both in Britain and abroad. When John Dale and his family travelled round the United States in a determined export drive promoting Denby ware, they found that the new tableware had to be renamed Camelot for the U.S. market to avoid confusion with a chain of Chevron gas stations. The name Camelot was chosen to reflect the popularity of the contemporary Broadway musical.

Betty Dale recalls how the American distributors had arranged for them to travel with other British exporters in the Flying Scotsman's Pullman carriages in which the Denby collection was displayed and transported from state to state in October 1969. She and her husband, with their daughter Susan, took part in a marathon whistle-stop tour, showing Denby ware in all the major cities, and visiting department stores to tell the Denby story. Working day and night, the family would set up their exhibition in the train when it visited one city, and take it down when the train moved overnight to the next destination. It was 'a killing pace', but the tour firmly established the Denby name in the States. Even the President's wife was said to have put Chevron/Camelot on a wedding present list. The family met many American celebrities during their tour and made a lasting impression on their American distributor, Lionel Simons, who was later to become the firm's Managing Director.

Susan Dale touring the U.S.A. on the Flying Scotsman, c.1969.

During the tour, John Dale played the part of a typical English gentleman, complete with bowler-hat, pin-striped suit and tightly rolled umbrella. In contrast, Susan Dale, then in her twenties, proved the ideal assistant in her Carnaby Street outfit and Vidal Sassoon haircut which complemented the Chevron style. Susan, worked for her father as a public relations officer and persuaded him to change from the traditional advertising agency to a firm more in tune with the current life-style. The change was a great success. The Dale family worked as a team during this time, helping in the London office and at trade shows. Quaintly, John never revealed his relationship to Betty and Susan to the clients, some of whom must have wondered how Betty Dale, ostensibly his secretary, was so successful in ensuring that the happy-go-lucky John invariably kept his important appointments. He was, of course, harassed over the breakfast table to underline the vital dates in his diary.

In 1969 the Pottery demonstrated its versatility by producing pre-formed ceramic cones for aero-engines in collaboration with Rolls Royce, setting up a separate business for the purpose.

Whilst visiting Italy during the 1960s, Norman Wood was shown a new type of electric, fast-firing kiln that could reduce production time to four-and-a-half hours, and obviate the need for weekend shift work. He realised that this would be invaluable and by 1967 the first such kiln in Britain was installed at Denby. Although he was in favour of modernisation, Norman realised that it could threaten standards of craftsmanship if taken to excess. Forty percent of Denby's production was mechanised but the Pottery still had more throwers and turners than any other pottery in Europe.

In 1969 the Denby Board was saddened to learn that, with the death of Major Charles Chittenden, the last surviving connection with the Bourne family had been severed. The London showroom in Thavies Inn House was extensively refurbished in 1970, and won the praise of the trade press as an example of good merchandising. To coincide with the opening, Eileen White, Norman Wood's versatile personal secretary, made an eighteen minute publicity film that was used for lectures and training purposes and successfully promoted the Denby image.

By 1970 the 'modernisation' of the factory that had been started in 1946 was regarded as complete. The company floated Denbyware Limited on the stock exchange but continued to trade as Joseph Bourne and Son until 1976. As Norman Wood had feared, the flotation brought in outside financial influences and constraints. There was a tendency to abandon the Denby tradition of good, innovative design for ware that was cheap to produce and aimed to satisfy a less discerning public. Denby's American distributor at that time was the Millward and Norman Company of Cincinatti whose President, Lionel Simons, was to become the major shareholder of Denbyware Ltd.

During this period, Denby's in-house designers often had different priorities from those of management with whom commercial demands sometimes seemed to outweigh aesthetic considerations. Management's problem was to reconcile these conflicting interests. It was to

David Yorath, c.1970.

Lionel Simons, c.1973.

Douglas Stone, c.1974.

Norman Wood's credit that he was usually successful in striking this delicate balance even in difficult financial circumstances.

Gill Pemberton continued to work on variations and developments of Chevron and Arabesque and created a new design every eighteen months. She was, however, becoming increasingly disillusioned and frustrated because many of her ideas were not accepted by management. She and Glyn were also very much aware of the fact that freelance designers were paid at a much higher rate than the in-house team.

David Yorath joined the company in 1970 as a designer, and produced studio pottery and tableware in the Denby tradition. In 1973 Kurt Franzen, a freelance designer from Denmark, created a range of highly successful oven-to-tableware that won national recognition. He also made a permanent claim to fame when he sculpted a portrait bust of Norman Wood, now on display in the Denby Museum.

By 1973, Lionel Simons had become the Managing Director of Denby with Norman Wood remaining as Chief Executive. Lionel Simons appointed Glyn and other long-serving staff as Directors in 1974. In his new role Glyn went to France, Poland and Portugal on the company's behalf, to oversee the development of new products in porcelain and glass. The other directors appointed included C. Delme Harrison, the Works Manager; Victor Thompson, the engineer and Douglas Stone, the chemist.

Denby employed many skilled and dedicated technicians who contributed substantially to the quality of the products. Denby is renowned for its superior glazes. Chemist, Percy Hunt, his father before him and his successor, Douglas Stone, created many hundreds of such glazes to produce the typical Denby look. Percy Hunt's father, Joe, is said to have ground all his glazes by hand using a mortar and pestle. Stoneware requires specialised machinery and Victor Thompson and his father not only adapted conventional pottery machinery, but, where necessary, made new equipment to meet the demands of Denby clay.

## FLEUR COWLES

In Limoges, France, Glyn co-operated with the remarkable Fleur Cowles to transfer her striking paintings onto porcelain tableware. Fleur was an American journalist, turned diplomat, turned artist who seemed to know everybody who was anybody on the international scene and worked successively for Presidents Hoover and Eisenhower. An internationally renowned artist, she was so prolific that it was even suspected she might have had a ghost-designer. Glyn was highly successful in creating saleable ware from Fleur's designs but her association with Denby was short-lived.

The political climate in Poland was unhappy at that time and Glyn kept his contacts with that country to a minimum. Furthermore, the experiment of using Polish

Fleur Cowles and Lionel Simons (centre) at the Exhibition of Jardin des Fleurs, 1976.

glass was not a commercial success. Portugal, on the other hand, was more to his taste and porcelain ware was produced for Denby in that country. In his continental work, Glyn was briefly assisted by another American designer, Sandi Tommela.

## EILEEN WHITE

Norman Wood's ability to recruit designers ideally suited to Denby was matched by his capacity for selecting appropriate administrative staff. This was reflected in his appointment of Eileen White. When the company needed office staff, a local headmaster recommended Eileen. Norman Wood immediately recognised her drive and potential. Eileen joined the company as an office junior in 1944 following in the steps of other members of her family who had been working for Denby from as early as the 1870s. One of her ancestors worked for Sarah Elizabeth Bourne and was mentioned in her will. After two years Eileen became Norman's secretary, working with him until he retired, before eventually rising to the position of Company Secretary in 1973 with a seat on the Board of Directors.

Her ability and dedication made her invaluable to the company and to Norman Wood. With his encouragement she became the company's historian and acquired many early pieces of Denby pottery which illustrate the firm's history. With these she set up a museum that has been installed in the Denby Visitors Centre. When the company was taken over by Coloroll in 1987, she ensured that many records were preserved and that the archives were removed to safe-keeping. An accomplished photographer, she also recorded the company's work on film. Like Sarah Elizabeth Bourne, Eileen became dedicated to the Denby Pottery and served it efficiently and loyally until her retirement in the 1980s.

# THE TABLEWARE REVOLUTION

Whereas in the previous decade contemporary style had been epitomised by the avant garde designs of Cheviot and Tigo Ware, the style of the 1960s was proclaimed in tableware produced at Denby and at Langley Pottery with designs by Gill Pemberton and Glyn Colledge. Many were the result of their collaboration with modifications of Gill's original shapes being marketed with decorations developed by Glyn.

At the beginning of the 1960s Kenneth Clark's original Gourmet shapes were modified and new glaze and decorative effects were created by Glyn.

**Studio** *tableware, issued in 1961, was decorated in a grey 'hare's fur' glaze with soft dark brown vertical lines and orange highlights on the knobs and handles. The orange dot which significantly enhanced the design is acknowledged by Glyn to have been the idea of Norman Wood.*

Two years later Glyn's tableware designs with sgraffito decoration were highly successful in America.

**Ode** *was glazed in antique gold and decorated with a white Greek Key pattern. It was awarded a Gold Medal for Excellence at the California State Fair, U.S.A.*

**Echo** *was finished in deep, misty-blue with a continuous spiralling pattern in white.*

Albert Colledge decorated modified Gourmet shapes with hand-painted leaf motifs.

**Shamrock** *bore a hand-painted trefoil in cool greens and browns on a white ground which was reminiscent of his famous Greenwheat.*

**Conifer**, *a Langley production, in olive-green and white, displayed a hand-painted cone and leaf in natural colours.*

**Lucerne** *created a modern impression in the mid-1960s. It was simply glazed in light brown with pale-blue interiors, at the Langley Pottery.*

These previous designs were a stage in the progression from the rounded, rustic shapes of Peasant Ware and Greenwheat to the revolutionary shapes created by Gill Pemberton.

**Shamrock**, advertising photograph, early 1960s.

## THE GILL PEMBERTON INFLUENCE

Gill's basic objective was to translate the traditional qualities of Denby stoneware into contemporary sculptural shapes which could be appreciated as objects of beauty and balance whilst retaining their functional qualities. Always working directly with the throwers, modellers and chemists, her ideas were translated directly to the clay. She was involved throughout in all the processes necessary to bring her ideas to fruition and has always acknowledged the skill and expertise of her co-workers. In a contemporary interview, Gill stated:

> 'Stoneware requires such a different technique, it's so basic...with stoneware clay you do things basically, spontaneously, urgently. China is so 'refined'. There's such a tremendous satisfaction in making...it's an emotional thing. To paraphrase a popular song of the day, 'I feel a shape coming on'. I see a design as a whole...perhaps it's a question of feeling more than seeing...feeling and a sensitivity for the earthy material with which you are working; I can throw and turn, but generally I get one of the experts to do it for me and together we produce a prototype. I actually modelled all the handles, spouts and new flatware myself.'

**Chevron**, *developed in 1961/2. was a radical design by a radical designer whose influence was reflected not only at Denby but throughout the pottery industry. It was based on the shape of a cheese jar which Gill had originally designed at Langley Pottery. Gill herself modelled every one of the seventy pieces included in the range, working closely with Hedley Parkin the modeller, Jim Seal the thrower and Albert Blancheon the turner. All casseroles and cups were hand-thrown initially and the flatware hand-jollied. After the natural roundness of the Manor Green and Greenwheat shapes, the throwers found it very difficult to achieve the vertical sides required for Chevron. The proportion of handles and spouts to the pot was ergonomically correct for balance and every item was appropriate for its use. Matt-glazed in khaki-green, its serrated pattern was created by the use of a small roller. The Chevron range, including her revolutionary metal-handled tea-kettle, was the epitomé of the 'Swinging Sixties'. It was accepted by the Design Centre and was put forward for a Duke of Edinburgh award.*

**Arabesque** *tableware was an extension of a small set of gift ware, designed by Gill Pemberton in 1962/3, which included three differently-sized jars, a large goblet and a salad bowl. The stylish jugs and cups of Arabesque had the same ergonomically correct handles as those on Chevron. A visit to Russia had inspired the exotic red and gold hand-painted decoration which she evolved and which was later executed by her decorator, 'Trish' Seal. Initially the pattern had been hand-painted directly onto the raw, unfired brown glaze but this was a difficult technique to perfect. Arabesque was produced for a short time using a decal or transfer print. The intention had been to call the range Samarkand but when the Portmeirion Pottery exhibited a range under that name, an alternative had to be found.*

# DENBY TABLEWARE

Brown Salt Glaze, Light Stone & White & Buff Stoneware.

Denby Ware

Chocolate Ware.

Emerald Ware.

British Fire-proof Ware. Green & Brown.

Celeste Ware.

Denby Chef Ware.

Advertising photograph illustrating early tableware, c.1920.

Denby Pottery

## Joseph Bourne & Son, Limited
Denby Pottery, Nr. Derby

*London Office & Showroom:*
**34, HOLBORN VIADUCT, E.C·1**

*In addition to the standard brown finish Denby ware
is now available in two attractive colours — Manor Green and Cottage Blue.*

JOSEPH BOURNE & SON LTD · DENBY POTTERY · NEAR DERBY

Above, promotional leaflets for **Cottage Blue**.

A group of **Cottage Blue** tableware mid-1930s.

The range of **Cottage Blue** shapes available.

# DENBY WARE

**Tea Pots : Coffee Jugs**
**Coffee Pots : Coffee Filters**

H. CHOCOLATE          L. CELESTE          D. DENBY COLOURS

M.G. MANOR GREEN          C.B. COTTAGE BLUE          J. EMERALD

E.P. EPIC GREEN          K. MAHOGANY          B.C. BLUE CONE

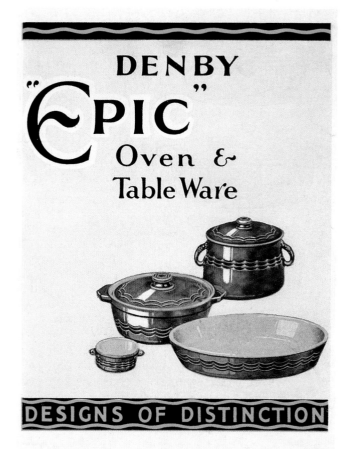

Epic

## Manor Green by Denby

Manor Green

Blue Cone

Advertising material illustrating tableware of the 1930s including the first hand-painted design, **Blue Cone**.

Hand-painted tableware with the **Flair** design, c.1947.

**Flair** hand-painted dish, c.1947.

A group of hand-painted tableware with the **Greenwheat** design, c.1956.

A factory promotional leaflet showing a selection of **Dovedale**, c.1956.

Hand-painted **Peasant** tableware, c.1954.

# DENBY *is at home in any setting . . .*

See how Denby oven and tableware fits the modern setting — beautifully designed, colourful, and so practical that meals can be served direct from the oven to the table in a matter of seconds. And if you are creating a new home you can buy Denby piece by piece without the restriction of a complete set that so often leaves you with too many of one item and not enough of others. Whatever your furnishings and decoration, this colourful Denby ware in Manor Green, Cottage Blue, or Homestead Brown will add charm to your table. See the range of

CASSEROLES, SOUP BOWLS, PLATES, CUPS, SAUCERS ETC

*Available at all leading China & Glass dealers and Departmental Stores throughout Great Britain*

**DENBY** OVEN AND TABLE WARE

*Write for illustrated leaflet to*

J O S E P H   B O U R N E   &   S O N   L T D . ,   ·   D E N B Y   P O T T E R Y ,   Nr.   D E R B Y

Denby . . . designed with you in mind

**DENBY**

Set the scene how you will — then bring it to life with the excitement of Denby designs and colours — for the art of entertaining lies as much in delighting the eye as in pleasing the palate.

*In addition to the Manor Green illustrated this range is available in Homestead Brown (brown and pale blue), Cottage Blue (dark blue and pale yellow) and Eclipse (black and white).*

*Write for illustrated leaflet 'C' with price list to:* JOSEPH BOURNE & SON LTD · DENBY POTTERY · NR. DERBY

Advertisments in a contemporary setting showing **Manor Green**, **Cottage Blue** and **Homestead Brown**. *House and Garden*, 1956.

243  Round casserole. 2 pt. 4 pt

244a  Oblong covered vegetable dish. 11˝.
245a Divided 11˝.

247  Oval sole dish. 10¼˝.

198  Gravy tureen . 200 Stand

135  Oval platter, 9¾˝. 12½˝.

203  Butter dish .

567  Hors d'oeuvre dish .4½˝. 8½˝.

161  Oatmeal bowl 6¼˝.

269  Cruet set . 5¾˝ Tray

165  Teapot ⅞ pt. 1½ pt.

166  Coffee jug 1 pt. 1½ pt.

170  Mug 12 oz

105  Egg cup

49  Bowl basin ½ pt. ⅓ pt

167  Open jug ½ pt. 1 pt

134  Plate 6½˝ 8˝ 10˝.

268  Tea cup . 133 Saucer.

Shape guide for the **Greenwheat** range, (see facing page).

**DENBY**

**dovedale**—*a recent addition to the Denby range*

can be seen at the Tea Centre, 22 Lower Regent Street, S.W.1, where *all* the Denby ranges of pottery are on view at an exhibition lasting from February 28th to March 17th. Denby potters will demonstrate daily the art of "Throwing" on the potters wheel.

Coloured illustrated Price Lists of all the Denby ranges are available on request from:—

JOSEPH  BOURNE  &  SON  LIMITED  ·  DENBY  POTTERY  ·  NR. DERBY

10                                    HOUSE & GARDEN

Advertisement showing the **Dovedale** range. *House and Garden*, 1956.

*Eclipse*—*and your table's dressed for dinner!*

made by **DENBY**

The coloured pottery accessories are from the Denby Boutique range

*Write for Illustrated folder:-*

JOSEPH BOURNE & SON LIMITED · DENBY POTTERY · NR. DERBY

24 HOUSE & GARDEN

*Galaware*

Designed and manufactured exclusively by
**JOSEPH BOURNE & SON LTD**
Denby Pottery, Nr. Derby, England

LONDON SHOWROOMS: 24 HOLBORN VIADUCT, LONDON, E.C.1

*Marguerita*
by **DENBY**

**Eclipse, Galaware, Tigo Ware** and **Marguerita**, contrasting styles in the 1950s – from the exuberant to the minimal.

Ode

Echo

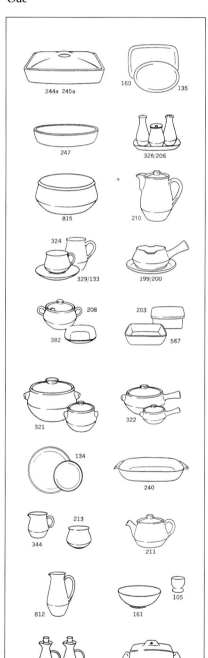

244a 245a    160    135

247    326/206

815    210

324    329/133    199/200

208    203

382    567

321    322

134    240

344    213    211

812    161    105

337    204

Studio

gourmet

designed by Kenneth Clark

Promotional leaflets showing the classic and award winning designs from the late 1950s and early 1960s and the range of shapes available.

Denby Pottery

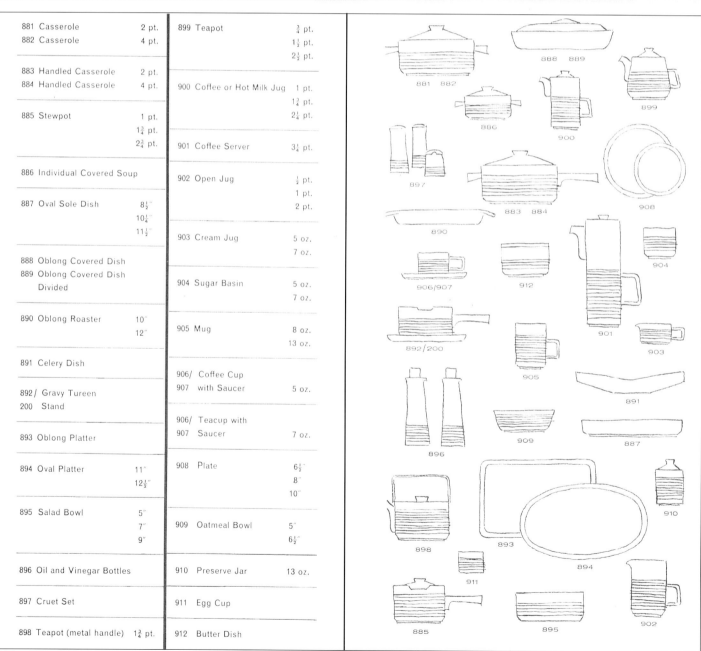

| | | | | | | |
|---|---|---|---|---|---|---|
| 881 | Casserole | 2 pt. | 899 | Teapot | | $\frac{3}{4}$ pt. |
| 882 | Casserole | 4 pt. | | | | $1\frac{1}{2}$ pt. |
| | | | | | | $2\frac{1}{2}$ pt. |
| 883 | Handled Casserole | 2 pt. | 900 | Coffee or Hot Milk Jug | | 1 pt. |
| 884 | Handled Casserole | 4 pt. | | | | $1\frac{3}{4}$ pt. |
| | | | | | | $2\frac{1}{4}$ pt. |
| 885 | Stewpot | 1 pt. | 901 | Coffee Server | | $3\frac{1}{4}$ pt. |
| | | $1\frac{3}{4}$ pt. | | | | |
| | | $2\frac{3}{4}$ pt. | 902 | Open Jug | | $\frac{1}{2}$ pt. |
| | | | | | | 1 pt. |
| 886 | Individual Covered Soup | | | | | 2 pt. |
| 887 | Oval Sole Dish | $8\frac{1}{2}''$ | 903 | Cream Jug | | 5 oz. |
| | | $10\frac{1}{4}''$ | | | | 7 oz. |
| | | $11\frac{1}{2}''$ | 904 | Sugar Basin | | 5 oz. |
| | | | | | | 7 oz. |
| 888 | Oblong Covered Dish | | | | | |
| 889 | Oblong Covered Dish Divided | | 905 | Mug | | 8 oz. |
| | | | | | | 13 oz. |
| 890 | Oblong Roaster | 10'' | 906/ | Coffee Cup | | |
| | | 12'' | 907 | with Saucer | | 5 oz. |
| 891 | Celery Dish | | 906/ | Teacup with | | |
| | | | 907 | Saucer | | 7 oz. |
| 892/ | Gravy Tureen | | | | | |
| 200 | Stand | | 908 | Plate | | $6\frac{1}{2}''$ |
| | | | | | | 8'' |
| 893 | Oblong Platter | | | | | 10'' |
| 894 | Oval Platter | 11'' | 909 | Oatmeal Bowl | | 5'' |
| | | $12\frac{1}{2}''$ | | | | $6\frac{1}{2}''$ |
| 895 | Salad Bowl | 5'' | | | | |
| | | 7'' | 910 | Preserve Jar | | 13 oz. |
| | | 9'' | | | | |
| 896 | Oil and Vinegar Bottles | | 911 | Egg Cup | | |
| 897 | Cruet Set | | 912 | Butter Dish | | |
| 898 | Teapot (metal handle) | $1\frac{3}{4}$ pt. | | | | |

The 1960s 'Design Revolution'. **Chevron** oven and tableware designed by Gill Pemberton, and a promotional leaflet showing the shapes available.

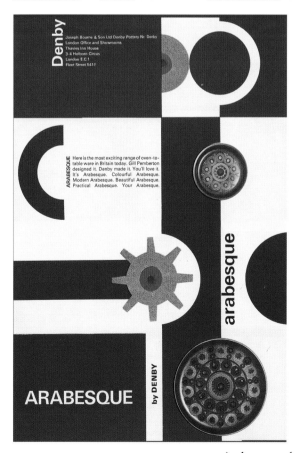

**Arabesque** – design co-ordination by Gill Pemberton, 1960s.

# Mayflower

# Canterbury

# Chatsworth

## SHERWOOD
### oven-to-table ware by Denby

Denby·the natural homemakers

Marketed by Denby in the mid-1960s under the name of Langley a 'natural homemaker' series, **Mayflower, Canterbury, Chatsworth** and **Sherwood**, were based on one set of shapes, whilst the traditional designs, **Manor Green, Cottage Blue** and **Homestead Brown**, retained their appeal.

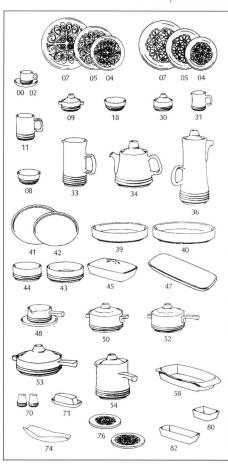

Advertising leaflet for the American market showing the floral design **Kismet**, and the stylized **Bokhara** together with the shapes available.

Tableware on display in the late 1960s.

**Romany**

**Minstrel** (back row) and **Gypsy**

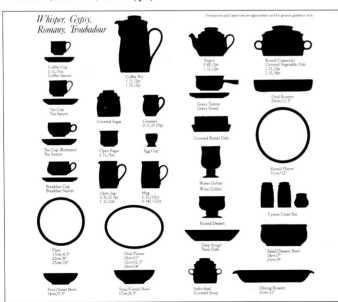

**Troubador.**

An early 1970s selection of contemporary styled tableware unique to Denby, and the range of shapes available.

Falstaff

Clouds

Westbury

Trees

Gourmet (second version)

Summit

Imaginative shapes and 'one-off' designs by freelance artists contrasted with the austere lines of **Gourmet** and **Summit.**

Potters Wheel

Rondo

Stone & Teak

Left and below, **Potters Wheel**.

The influence of the traditional studio potter is contrasted with the sophisticated shapes of **Rondo**.

"Palomar"

"Shasta"

"Sierra Pinta"

"Mauna Loa"

"Cimarron"

Sonnet

Whisper

Sahara    Fjord    Corfu

The Naturals Collection

**Denby Days**

Russet

Rochester

By the end of the 1970s ware was strictly functional, simply glazed and with the minimum of decoration.

**Jardin des Fleurs**

Eileen White with the original painting by Fleur Cowles, c.1975.

**Jardin des Fleurs**

**Jardin des Fleurs**

**Jungle** plates

"Take some more tea," the March Hare said to Alice...

"Well, this is grand!" said *Alice*. A mad *Tea Party*...

**Wonderland**

...so she sat on, with eyes closed and half believed herself in Wonderland...

**Denby.**

The White Rabbit blew three blasts on his trumpet...

..."so please *Your Majesty*," said Alice.

"When I'm a *Duchess*," she said to herself.

**Dreaming**

In a Wonderland they lie, Dreaming as the days go by...

All in the *Golden Afternoon*...

..."you have no idea what a delightful thing a *Quadrille* is."

*"Contrariwise,"* continued Tweedledee.

**Denby.**

The Looking Glass Collection

**Once Upon A Time Collection.** Left to right: **Dreamweavers**, 1975/6; **Apple Mouse**, 1982; **Safari**, 1979.

The Country Fayre Collection, Cotswold (second version), 1973.

The Country Fayre Collection, Chiltern, 1975.

Once Upon A Time Collection. Boxed giftware.

The Renaissance Collection. Left, **Castile**, and right, **Seville**, 1975.

## The Chateau Collection

Savoy, 1982.

Dauphine, 1982.

Provence, 1982.

Chantilly, 1982.

## The Artisan Collection

Midnight 1983.

Reflections, 1985.

Camelot, 1986.

Decoy Duck, 1987.

The Sherwood Collection

**Daybreak**, 1983.

**Twilight**, 1983.

**Blue Dawn**, 1984.

**Summerfields**, 1984.

**Images**, 1987.

**Maplewood**, 1987.

**Damask**, 1991.

**Imperial Blue**, 1989.

The Stratford Collection

**Sandalwood,** 1986.

**Oberon,** 1986.

The Discovery Collection

The Columbia Series

**Chorus,** 1987.

**Tivoli,** 1990.

**Saturn,** 1987.

**Parisienne,** 1990.

**Mercury,** 1988.

**Mandarin,** 1991.

**The Sovereign Shape**. Left, **Marrakesh**, 1992, and right, **Shiraz**, 1993.

**The Meridian Shape, Luxor**, 1995.

**The Meridian Shape, Boston Spa**, 1997.

The Sovereign Shape. Left, **Baroque**, 1992, and right, **Regatta**, 1993.

The Meridian Shape. Left, **Boston**, 1995, and right, **Greenwich**, 1994.

Casual Tableware. **Harlequin,** 1992, and **Spice**, 1993 (**Harlequin** teapots centre, **Spice** teapot far right).

Casual Tableware. **Metz**, 1996.

Casual Tableware. **Greenwich** platter, 1994 and **Metz** platters, 1996 and 1997.

**1990s Mugs**

**Gatsby Deco**
(top row left).
**Batik** (top row,
second left).

**Gatsby Stripe**
(second row left).

**Harlequin**, **Spice**
and **Flame**.

'Trish' Seal, decorator 1970s.

From 1964 onwards, contemporary tableware shapes were designed by Gill Pemberton and produced at the Langley Pottery. Each series was unified by a typically Denby glaze, with colour and individuality achieved by the application of a stylised, hand-painted floral decoration to the plates and bowls. Some of these surface patterns were by Gill, some by Glyn. Mechanical variations produced by other potteries followed the trend set by Denby but lacked the vigour and artistry of the hand-painted Denby originals.

**Mayflower** *with its homespun quality, was produced in 1964 and especially named for the American market. Popular in this country throughout the 1960s it was the forerunner of many other stylised floral patterns. Entirely the work of Gill Pemberton the dark-brown ribbed coffee pots and jugs had an unusual projecting side handle. The plates displayed an upright spray of three flowers in shades of yellow, gold and brown. In the prototypes these were painted directly onto the raw glaze but due to production constraints they were later painted on to the fired glaze.*

Three tableware series, each featuring a stylised floral pattern designed by Glyn, were marketed on Gill's Mayflower shapes.

**Sherwood** *was glazed in dark olive-green with a green, rust, ivory and blue flower freely painted onto the light stone-coloured plates. It was first produced in 1966.*

**Canterbury** *was likened in an advertisement of the day to 'the colour of warm sunlight on a sandstone wall'. Unlike Mayflower, the teapots, jugs and bowls had conventional handles instead of the single bar. The formalised pattern of flowers, buds and leaves in browns and golds covered the plates.*

**Chatsworth** *in a rich blue, with white, blue-rimmed plates, decorated with a large blue/grey flower, centrally placed.*

An Eastern influence is reflected in two designs based on modified Chevron shapes in which prominent ridges encircle the lower part of each teapot, jug, cup and bowl.

**Bokhara,** *created by Gill in 1967, had the same exotic quality as Arabesque and was hand-painted in rich dark colours. Most unusually, curving scrolls reminiscent of Islamic art, were actually sculpted into the plate. The plates were labour-intensive and expensive to produce. Gill Pemberton had again produced exciting pottery that was entirely appropriate for its time, for Denby clay and for Denby expertise. Two or three years later a simpler screen-printed pattern was created by Glyn and applied to plates for the American market.*

Norman Wood and Glyn had been to Stoke-on-Trent to study the latest methods of screen printing. As none was considered appropriate for Denby, Glyn evolved both his own technique and equipment. The prints were transferred via a plastic sieve and its frame was dispensed with to allow greater flexibility and accuracy.

The red centre of each flower 'lifted' and highlighted the pattern. There are three theories for its appearance. Firstly, Gill placed it there herself. Secondly, it arrived accidentally when a small piece of glaze dropped onto a pot during an experimental firing. Thirdly, Norman Wood was considering a prototype for Arabesque, which was then minus its red spot. Taking a red biro to the pot and touching the centre of each flower, he said, 'That's what is needed'. As Gill says today, 'It was probably a combination of all three factors – it evolved, as all good designs must.'

A large circular 'chop' plate showed the design to perfection. Gill had been told that it would be impossible to produce such a large piece, but, with the help of Hedley Parkin, she ensured, by gauging the right balance and weight, that it would be quite viable. Today it is the decorative aspect of these pieces which commands the attention of collectors.

**Patrician** *was modelled on the catering ware shapes which Gill had designed at college and which had been manufactured as such at Langley. 'Langley needed a Chevron - hence my catering ware was revamped'. With vertical lines round the lower half of the ware it was moulded and jollied in 1964 at the Langley factory. Initially it was glazed in antique gold and white and later in turquoise and in yellow, colours popular in the mid-1960s.*

**Kismet,** *issued in 1969 in America* (**Bokhara Cluster** *in England*), *was glazed in a deep rich blue. Plates displayed a hand-painted pattern of five stylised daisy heads with yellow centres designed by Glyn. It was later issued as a decal.*

Another tableware series was in complete contrast.

**Summit,** *a cool, stylish design by Gill and Glyn, was simply glazed in off-white and brown on Arabesque shapes.*

During the 1970s both Glyn and Gill Pemberton were responsible for new ranges of tableware but ideas which were artistically correct were now having to be modified and replaced by designs governed by financial constraints. For example, Gill's outstanding decoration for Falstaff plates was rejected by the management on the grounds of cost. Fortunately for the collector however, Glyn's hand-painted, impressionistic alternative was a masterpiece of simplicity. Similarly, the original floral design for Gypsy tableware which had included a butterfly and a tree, was judged to be too time-consuming to produce. Generally speaking, pretty flowers do not sit appropriately on the strong Denby stoneware but those placed on Glyn's shapes in the 1970s were the exception that proved the rule. Trish Seal was closely involved with these designs.

**Gypsy** *consisted of shapes in which the traditional and modern style were harmonised and large, dusky-pink, wild roses complemented the gently curving shapes. It had a lasting appeal and, five years later, was featured as an example of good contemporary design in The Design Centre Tableware Buyers Guide of 1977.*

**Minstrel** *was a later version of Gypsy with gold and yellow flowers.*

**Troubador,** *a work of art in its simplicity, line and colour, displayed hand-painted magnolias and leaves in soft greens and browns with touches of pink.*

**Romany,** *in contrast, was plainly glazed in old gold encircled by a dark-brown running glaze which created an irregular curtain effect. It was 'invented' in the glaze development workshop. One Saturday morning, Jim Moss accidentally mixed the wrong proportions of coloured glazes which he then applied to a trial piece to await Glyn's approval. On Monday morning when the firing was completed, Glyn was delighted with the glaze effect and surprised by the unusual and unexpected encrustations which had formed. The glazing team always claimed Romany as 'theirs'.*

Two in-house decorators each produced a design for Glyn's shapes.

**Whisper** *by Thelma Hague was marketed as a 'romantic design' in white, bearing lightly-sketched pale-blue flowers with brown centres.*

**Pot Pourri** *by Trish Seal was decorated with a transfer print of three large flowers on a light ground. They were either yellow and orange or blue and white (see also* **Shasta***).*

Diana Woodcock-Beckering, c.1970.

Gill's strength lay in the originality of her tableware shapes and, in the early 1970s, co-operating with Glyn, she produced three very different series.

**Falstaff** *was a striking design alternative to the soft lines and colours of Gypsy and Troubador and to the rustic tableware offered by freelance designers. Marketed in 1971/2, it consisted of extravagantly rounded shapes decorated with a dominant purple glaze. The large, freely-painted anemones in brilliant scarlet and purple set on white purple-rimmed plates were the inimitable work of Glyn in the modern idiom.*

**Westbury** *was issued on hybrid shapes based on Gill's earlier work. It was Glyn's idea to cover the light-coloured body of the ware in a shaded slip which proved to be an ideal background for the gold, pink, and brown flowers with which Gill decorated the plates and bowls. This bold contemporary pattern reflected the best in folk art.*

**The Artisan Range** (first version).*Stackable tableware, was fashioned by Gill Pemberton in three days in response to a rush order from America. Glyn worked on the glaze and decorative effects, of which there were six variations:*

**Shasta** and **San Gabriel** *were contrasting floral designs, the three flowers of Shasta were in yellow and two shades of blue and San Gabriel was decorated with a large stylised flower head in shades of brown and gold with an orange centre.*

**Maunaloa** and **Palomar** *each displayed coloured concentric rings, the former in ochre and green and the latter in ochre and brown with an orange centre.*

**Sierra** and **Cimarron** *were plainly glazed in speckled-white and dark-brown respectively.*

In the 1970s freelance designers appeared briefly, made a significant contribution and then moved on.

**Trees** *by Diana Woodcock-Beckering featured a striking hand-painted design of black, stylised trees, set against clouds and a purple sky. Gill's original Chevron shapes, including a metal-handled teapot, were most appropriate for this contemporary design. Trained at the Royal College of Art, Diana worked mainly with Glyn between 1969 and 1971.*

Trees, c.1970.

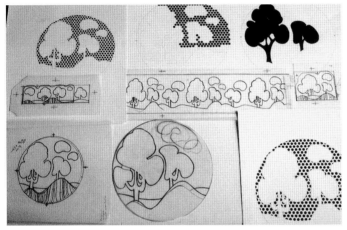

Working drawings for **Trees**.

**Potters Wheel** *designed in 1973 by David Yorath had a simple oatmeal and brown pattern of concentric circles in which the central area was glazed in either a rust, yellow, green or blue.*

**Stone And Teak** *was a complementary range of condiment sets by him in which stoneware and wood were combined.*

**Gourmet** (second version) *designed by Kurt Franzen, was illustrated in the Design Centre Buyers Guide of 1974 in recognition of its quality. Its strong compact shapes and recessed lids were emphasised by circular ridges. Glazed in vanilla and in chocolate-brown, it was an innovative alternative to the traditional Manor Green, Cottage Blue and Homestead Brown cookware currently on offer.*

Throughout the 1960s, when a new tableware design had proved to be popular with the public, Denby would reissue or modify the shapes, apply a new surface decoration and so launch a new line. It was far more cost-effective to change the external decoration than to produce a new set of shapes. The creation of a 'collection' of shapes to be reissued over a period of years with new glaze or decorative effects became company policy in the 1970s.

## THE COLLECTIONS

### The Country Fayre Collection
*Designed by Glyn, the rustic shapes, partly hand-textured and glazed in dark-brown were reminiscent of the Chocolate Ware made in the last century.*

**Cotswold** (second version), **Sable** *and* **Chiltern** *were each glazed in brown but two of the designs displayed a curving spray of flowers and leaves on the white, brown rimmed plates and bowls. In 1973 Cotswold was freely painted in soft browns and gold and two years later the well-defined flowers of Chiltern were coloured in pastel-blue, pink and ochre.*

By 1975 foreign influences were affecting Denby's output. Porcelain production was studied in France and Portugal and designers were expected to apply their newly gained knowledge to Denby stoneware. As a direct result, Gill Pemberton had designed the refined Renaissance Collection.

### The Renaissance Collection
*This elegant series of fine-quality stoneware decorated with rouletting was created by Gill Pemberton for the American market at Lionel Simons' request. The goblet-shaped cups, bowls and jugs with gently curving, concavo-convex outlines created the appearance of fine china whilst maintaining the strength and durability for which Denby pottery was renowned. The first two decorative glazes chosen by Gill Pemberton were highly successful and were still in production ten years later. In contrast, other designs which were decorated in 'romantic colours' with tiny pastel flowers had a short life.*

**Seville** *and* **Castile** *were glazed in light brown and white and in blue and white respectively.*

**Medici** *was glazed in white.*

**Avignon, Verona** *and* **Lorraine** *were floral designs on a pale stone ground. Avignon was garlanded and Verona sprigged with tiny flowers, whilst a bouquet of mauve and blue flowers on Lorraine attracted a butterfly.*

**Venice** *and* **Alsace,** *in green and white, and in clerical grey and white were later variations, of which there were several.*

The best of Denby pottery was always design-led. By the mid-1970s too many innovations and diversifications were being introduced by a management which was taking much of the power from the designers and denying their vision.

## DECORATIVE WARE

The production of decorative ware was dominated by another major series by Glyn Colledge. Marketed as an expensive, prestige product, Glynbourne sold well for over ten years. It was not until the 1970s that new exotic Eastern designs by Gill Pemberton and David Yorath were created. Simultaneously David Yorath was displaying his skill and craftsmanship by producing a range of highly individual, signed studio pottery vases. Trish Seal worked with him in creating some of the decorative surface effects.

**Glynbourne** *designed by Glyn between 1960/1 included large hand-thrown bowls, vases, jugs. To the natural shapes created by generations of craftsmen, Glyn added his own, individual sense of design and harmony. Each matt-glazed shape was hand-painted in greens and browns with its own overall abstract pattern of leaves.*

Glyn designed the ware, working directly with the throwers and decorators and also organised its progress throughout the technical stages of production. Glynbourne was studio pottery in the true Denby tradition, to which Glyn had already contributed with his early designs. It is still keenly sought after and collected today.

**Lamp Bases** *with floral and leaf decorations, similar in style to Glyn Ware were designed by Glyn from 1963 onwards. Some were made specifically for the Bristol Company of Birmingham and were neither signed by Glyn nor marked Denby.*

**Flamstead** *vases, jugs and bowls by Glyn, some featuring prominent strap-like handles, were glazed in light brown and decorated by Glyn in the contemporary style. Each piece was encircled by three adjacent bands of small concentric or spiralling circles, tube-lined in white and highlighted with an orange or green centre. Issued in 1966/7 it was named after the first Astronomer Royal, John Flamstead, who was born at Crowtrees, Denby Village, in 1646.*

Unlike many British manufacturers in the 1920s, when interest in Egyptology was at its height following the opening of King Tutenkhamun's tomb in 1922, there

Three studio vases by David Yorath. The abstract painting on vases 1 and 3 were his work, but vase 2 was decorated with flowers and 'cut out' by Trish Seal.

appears to have been little, if any, reaction from Denby. Was the production of Donald Gilbert's Cleopatra bowl and vase in the early 1930s a delayed response? Fifty years later, however, Denby was more in tune with current trends and by the time the Egyptian Exhibition was opened at the Victoria and Albert Museum in 1972, two topical designs were already in production.

A factory promotional leaflet, c.1960.

Egyptian Wall Plaques *based on items in the Exhibition were issued in the early 1970s as a limited edition of 5000. The plates were sculpted by Gill herself working in conjunction with John Challons, the modeller. The hand-painted scenes of Egyptian antiquity in soft ochres and browns were the result of co-operation between Gill and the skilled paintress Trish Seal. Out of six prototypes, only four were put into production. They were boxed in pairs and each accompanied by a parchment scroll.*

Minaret *by David Yorath drew on Middle Eastern sources for inspiration. Introduced in the early 1970s in shades of ochre, gold and brown, its complex Persian-styled patterns encircled the central area whilst the upper and lower parts of the cylindrical vases were simply ridged. A version was available in blue. Many pieces were hand-painted by Audrey Cole-Parker.*

# REPRODUCTIONS

In the 1960s as a reaction to the contemporary designs of the previous decade, Denby reverted to its traditional past with a series of nineteenth-century reproductions for the American market.

Village *issued in 1961/2, although it included six of the Reform Cordial Flasks, consisted mainly of functional items.*

Ten years later a selection of early shapes which had initially been sprigged and salt-glazed was marketed using original pots as the basis for moulds which were then decorated with a modern glaze which merely simulated the original salt-glaze.

Antique Reproductions *included a Toby jug, a puzzle jug, a hunting jug and a covered game-pie dish. A pistol-shaped spirit flask and the Reform Cordial Flasks, with the exception of Queen Adelaide and Lord Grey, were also reproduced.*

The heyday of Denby decorative ware was drawing to a close.

Antique Reproductions.

# CHAPTER 10

# DIVERSIFICATION AND THE WILDERNESS YEARS
## 1976 - 1986

A major change of name took place in 1976 – Joseph Bourne and Son Ltd. and Langley Pottery Ltd. were united to form Denby Tableware Ltd. Glyn Colledge was made New Products Manager and, as such, he was involved in taking transfers made in France to Portugal for application onto porcelain. The decorative porcelain thus produced was then marked with the Denby stamp and exported, mainly to the United States.

Under Denby Tableware Ltd. the company's products were diversified. 'A completely co-ordinated table top' was the objective. Cutlery was produced with ceramic handles designed by Gill Pemberton with metal work by her husband. This gained an award at the Ideal Home Exhibition. At first the blades were produced in Sheffield, but, later, more cheaply in Taiwan. Glassware was made for the company in Poland and Portugal and teak table accessories were imported from Malaysia. The company even imported 'distressed' Colonial-American furniture but, as this was much too large for the British home, the venture was unsuccessful. The experiment in diversification was comparatively short-lived.

By 1976 the company's diversification projects were turning profits into losses and Denby's fortunes were on a downward curve. There were grave disagreements on the Denby Board between Lionel Simons and the other members. On the 1st April 1977, Lionel Simons tendered his resignation. Robert Huddie was appointed as the new Managing Director. Norman Wood retired as an executive director but kept his position on the company's board and was retained as a consultant. In 1979 a new young artist, Claire Bernard, joined Glyn and Gill but, despite their combined talents, the company floundered in a sea of unwise policy decisions. During this period Gill was made Director of Design but given no additional power or resources.

The Thatcherite 'revolution' was, by 1981, well under way in British industry and, in an entrepreneurial bid to expand its holdings and diversify its products, the Crown House Engineering Group bought Denby Tableware Ltd. despite the resistance of the Denby Board. Gill Pemberton had, by this time, become completely disillusioned by what she saw as the company's lack of a design policy – she felt that 'design was not understood or valued' – and submitted her resignation.

The incoming Crown House owners set about 'rationalising' the company's organisation. They sold the historic Langley site which was then bulldozed for development, much to the distress of the staff and collectors of Langley ware. The equipment and staff were transferred to Denby but one hundred and twenty employees were made redundant and the tradition and dynamics built up over more than one hundred years were,

Robert Huddie with antiques expert Arthur Negus, c.1977.

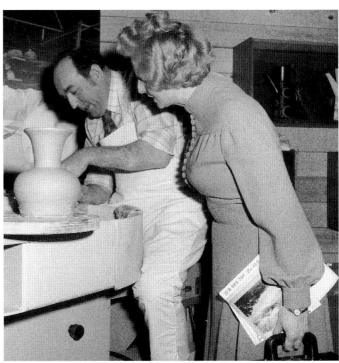

Margaret Thatcher watches Jim Seal at work, 1970s.

Glenys Taylor decorating mugs for the wedding of Prince Charles and Princess Diana, 1981.

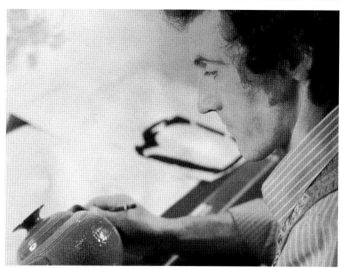

Robin Pavitt in his studio, 1980s.

inevitably, lost. Management and design functions were centralised at the Crown House headquarters in distant Flitwick, Bedfordshire, leaving the Denby site virtually rudderless and adrift. Day-to-day management remained in the capable hands of Fred Cooper (who was now Managing Director) and Eileen White, but overall control was exercised by remote Crown House executives who were known as Function Heads. By this time, the company seemed to have lost its sense of direction and design.

Crown House was demanding a new design every three months compared with the Denby tradition of developing designs over two years. These new marketing concepts were alien to the Denby designers who were continually under pressure to increase their output. Two new designers were employed, Robin Pavitt (from 1982-1985), and Rodney Endean (from 1985-1987). The company's export trade began to deteriorate and for six years there was no capital investment in new plant or equipment.

The atmosphere at Denby was so unhappy that, in 1983, Glyn Colledge decided to take early retirement. Unlike Gill, who had resigned in some anger, Glyn negotiated a satisfactory settlement to compensate him for his lifetime of distinguished service. In a typically unassuming manner he left the site so quietly that, '...no-one knew I had gone'.

Denby Fine Porcelain (Portugal) brought out in 1985, after Glyn had left, was one of the products of his pioneer work in that country, but even that failed to stem the flow of declining profits.

Richard Eaton first came to Denby as a student in 1986 to gain the practical experience necessary to complete his Master of Arts degree in ceramics. By that time Crown House plc had owned the Pottery for five years and the design department had been seriously neglected. The studio was too far from the kilns and the throwers, and the Crown House managers were prescribing the limited number of colours and glazes that could be used. Richard has since described these as the 'wilderness years' but,

nevertheless, some good designs were produced by Robin Pavitt and Rodney Endean.

As a project Richard Eaton was asked to design a range of gift ware. Using traditional skills 'that had nearly been forgotten' during the Crown House period, he created the expressive Origins decorative ware which was not actually put in into production until 1987 – a remarkable achievement for a student designer. Enthusiastic about his work, he stayed with Denby beyond the usual ten weeks and even returned for occasional days to monitor progress.

Towards the end of the 1980s, design generally was being influenced by the high-tech, black leather and chrome of the Habitat school. At Denby, however, whilst the tradition of good design had once been paramount it was now, unfortunately, overtaken by the exclusively profit-orientated design policy of Crown House. Eventually, Crown House made the entire Denby design team redundant.

In the successful sixties and early seventies Denby had employed nearly one thousand staff at its various sites, but by now the numbers were below four hundred. Denby was very low on the Crown House list of priorities and the situation there had deteriorated to such an extent that the company either had to be sold or closed down. The weakened company was ready for takeover by another predator, the highly successful Coloroll Group. Coloroll had already engulfed several potteries including Biltons, Royal Winton and The Staffordshire Pottery, to expand its homeware empire.

# COLLECTIONS

Although some excellent new wares were produced during this period, designers were not being given the backing necessary to allow them to develop their own ideas. They were continually reminded of financial constraints and of the need to respond to market forces.

In 1976, Gill Pemberton gained national recognition with a range of oven-to-tableware but eventually her tableware shapes were modified, and whilst successful on a practical level, they were in a different category from her original designs. In 1976 output was prolific and varied and included many of the successful designs from the 1960s and early 1970s.

Three new series of oven-to-table stoneware were designed by Gill Pemberton.

**Rochester** *was simply glazed in a rich green and white on modern shapes that retained a rustic appeal.*

**Russett**, *a functional design with a cream speckled ground and wide concentric rings in chocolate-brown, was aimed to satisfy the hotel and catering trade.*

**Rondo** *was a significant series in which Gill Pemberton made an original design statement. She created strong cylindrical shapes, with recessed lids and dominant toothed decoration. Original glazes in dark-brown and a greeny-grey created by the use of a white glaze over a reactive iron slip were devised by one of Denby's most skilled craftsmen, Douglas Stone, working in consultation with Gill. Together they created special effects which emphasised the rims of the pots and the incised decoration, thus illustrating the way in which Denby designs continued to be enhanced by the unique glazes which were formulated and prepared in-house.*

Rondo was the only design Gill actually drew for Denby. There was no alternative, as she was at home looking after her children who were ill, and no clay was to hand. Rondo was featured in the Victoria and Albert Museum exhibition, 'The Way We Are Now – designs for interiors, 1950 to the Present Day'. Her drawings are now to be found in the Print Department of the Museum.

**Madrigal** *was a variation of Rondo minus the toothed decoration, glazed in white and beige edged in brown.*

**Sonnet**, *another version of Rondo, was glazed in mink-brown.*

## Denby Days
*This series of tableware exemplified the trend by which Gill Pemberton's shapes were adapted and plainly glazed. In 1979 it was sold in boxed sets:*

**Corfu, Fjord** and **Sahara** *were glazed in blue, with a purple rim, green with a pale-green rim edged in darker green and in cream, edged with brown respectively. Sahara was also marketed through a mail order firm.*

There was one exception to the trend.

**Clouds**, *a one-off set of tableware was described in an advertising leaflet as 'Denby at its most contemporary and aimed to please the more avant-garde'. It displayed an intricate design of richly-coloured, formalised clouds.*

A factory had been found in Portugal in 1975 which could manufacture a specially strengthened porcelain and as a result a new porcelain collection was masterminded by Glyn in his role as New Products Manager. With the exception of quality the ware bore no resemblance to what most people would recognise as Denby style. It was innovation and diversification carried to extremes.

## The Looking Glass Collection.
*Three sets of bright white porcelain tableware shapes made in Portugal were decorated with vivid coloured flowers, trailing leaves and butterflies. Lewis Carroll's story of Alice in Wonderland was reflected in the names of the variations:*

**Alice, Wonderland, Tea Party, Dreaming, Duchess, Your Majesty, Quadrille, Contrariwise, Golden Afternoon.**

**Tiger Lily** *featured the pale-orange flower set against a squared trellis fence.*

## FLEUR COWLES.

Brilliant white porcelain made in France was decorated with designs based on original paintings by the American artist Fleur Cowles. Glyn supervised all the technical aspects of her work which had to comply with stringent rules laid down by the United States Government. New skills were needed to translate her colourful designs onto porcelain. Colour slides of her paintings were made into transfers which were then printed by Johnson Matthey and applied at Denby.

**Jardin Des Fleurs** *was based on simple, stark white porcelain shapes made at Limoges which were an excellent foil for her brilliantly-coloured botanically correct flowers. Different items of tableware were decorated with only a part of her painting. Four plates, for example, would each illustrate different flowers from a different section of one picture – a simple but original approach effected by Glyn Colledge.*

**Jungle Plates** *in jewel-like colours defined a profusion of flowers, foliage and trees in Fleur Cowles' tropical jungles. Only careful scrutiny would reveal the watchful presence of a tiger on these decorative items.*

**Mugs.** An increasingly casual life-style required a less formal approach to tableware and gradually the number and variety of mugs offered for sale was increased.

## Six of The Best
*'Trish' Seal designed six mugs, four of which were hand-painted with simple, stylised leaf patterns and two were encircled by small upright flowers.*

Examples of transfer-printed mugs, c.1986.

A silk-screen workshop opened in 1977, was supervised by Tony Richardson. For the first time, Denby introduced its own transfer prints which were used to decorate mugs and children's ware.

**London Scenes.** *St. Pauls, The Tower, Horse Guards Parade and Hampton Court were depicted on a series of mugs designed by Gill Pemberton.*

Three sets of mugs with a naturalist theme were based on delicate watercolours by the artist John Morland.

**Birds of a Feather** *A blue tit, a chaffinch, a robin and a wren.*

**Seasons of Mellow Fruitfulness.** *Apples, blackberries, pears and plums.*

**Wild Animals** *Chimpanzees, lions, pandas and tigers were introduced in 1980.*

A complementary series was based on fine scenic illustrations by Claire Bernard, one appearing on microwave ware in 1990.

**The Seasons** *Spring, Summer, Autumn, Winter.*

Thelma Hague painting the **Fresco** vase in the mid-1980s.

## CHILDREN'S POTTERY

**Once Upon a Time** *Three sets of children's pottery explored the story-book theme:*

**Dream Weavers**, *in pink and blue, created by Trish Seal in 1975/6, was the first in the series. In idyllic, open-air scenes, one child flew a kite and another sat fishing.*

**Safari** *by Thelma Hague was marketed in 1979. A crazy train travelling on a switch-back railway transported a giraffe, a lion and other animal friends in holiday mood.*

**Apple Mouse** *in pink and blue, by Barbara Sharp completed the series in 1982 when a comical mouse sat under an apple-laden tree by the side of a toadstool house.*

In the years immediately prior to the Coloroll takeover in 1987 the range of shapes and decorative effects had proliferated to such an extent that in 1983/4 Denby was making a dozen individual sets of tableware shapes and marketing four complete collections, each with a different range of decorative effects. Yet another new collection of shapes was launched as late as 1986.

In 1984 work by previous designers continued to be an important part of production. Homestead Brown on shapes by Donald Gilbert; Arabesque and Sahara by Gill Pemberton; Gypsy Troubador , Romany and Cotswold by Glyn Colledge; and Potters Wheel by David Yorath, together with more recent designs: Bakewell; Country Cuisine; Falling Leaves; Memories; Romance; and Windflower. Incredibly all these ranges were being produced simultaneously.

**Bakewell** *was traditionally shaped, glazed in dark-brown and hand-painted with a bold ochre flower and stylised leaf sprays.*

**Country Cuisine** *with angled sides was glazed in coffee-brown, dark-brown and white.*

**Falling Leaves** *was glazed in white with an overall, ordered pattern of three lobed leaves and three dots in pink.*

**Memories** *displayed a spray of pale flowers and leaves in soft ochre shades merging into the cream background.*

**Romance** *was glazed in turquoise, grey and white on Gill's earlier Madrigal shapes. In stylistic contrast the plates and bowls were decorated, according to advertising material, with 'great delicacy' and an 'almost ethereal floral effect'.*

**Windflower** *delicately stylised, freely hand-painted in pink, cream and orange with fine brown leaves, was set on an off-white ground.*

# THE COLLECTIONS

## The Chateau Collection

*The name of the collection and the fineness of its stoneware reflected the influence of French porcelain. Some of the decorative effects were strong and bold, others pale and pretty:*

**Savoy** and **Provence** *were glazed in strong colours. Savoy, by Thelma Hague, with its silhouetted, bare-branched tree, furrowed field and red roofed cottage had been the inspiration for the Collection in 1982. Provence, in contrast, was simply glazed in a speckled brown with white interiors.*

**Chantilly, Brittany, Dauphine** and **Normandy** *were pale designs on a pale background. With the exception of the intricate lacy pattern on Chantilly by Claire Bernard, the floral designs were by Thelma Hague.*

## The Artisan Collection (second version)
*This series was based in 1983/4 on Robin Pavitt's original shapes. A cottage-loaf shaped casserole was designed by Thelma Hague:*

**Midnight, Sundance** and **Reflections** *were transfer-printed. Midnight, in deep blue with a stylised floral pattern was by Thelma Hague. Sundance, in pale-green with a scalloped design, was followed in 1985 by the daisies of Reflections by Claire Bernard.*

**Greystone, Camelot** and **Pampas**, *smoky grey brown with white in 1983, soft olive-green with cream in 1986 and coffee-brown with cream in 1987 followed in the rustic tradition.*

## The Sherwood Collection
*A successful new set of tableware with rounded shapes was designed by Robin Pavitt in 1983:*

**Daybreak, Twilight, Blue Dawn** and **Summerfields** *were decorated with floral transfer prints. The first two designs were drawn by Claire Bernard and were so well received that, in 1984, the shapes were marketed as a Collection with the addition of Blue Dawn by Claire and Summerfields by Thelma Hague.*

## The Renaissance Collection
*Castile and Seville, the first designs to be issued were also the last, surviving until 1987.*

Denby Village, c.1979.

## The Stratford Collection
*With shapes rooted in the 1970s this series, by Rodney Endean, was introduced in 1986, to be discontinued after only one year:*

**Oberon** and **Sandalwood** *were decorated very differently. Oberon by Thelma Hague, was glazed in dark olive-green with a simple pattern of stylised berries in orange and pale-green, whilst Sandalwood, in a rich cream, displayed a delicate floral transfer print freely drawn by Claire Bernard.*

Too many pretty, pale flowers graced pastel tableware as Denby attempted to compete with the floral trends prevalent in Stoke-on-Trent. However beautiful the individual floral designs of Claire Bernard and Thelma Hague, the direction of Denby stoneware was diverted as it followed the floral path. Glyn Colledge had left, Gill Pemberton had left, there was no designer to provide the vision and stimulate the creativities of a design team. There was no design team. Denby was adrift.

# DECORATIVE WARE

Gradually the strong tradition of individually hand-decorated ware was phased out. In 1978 Glyn created his last decorative series, Savannah, and Gill Pemberton designed the striking Cascade which relied on luminous glazes for its appeal.

**Savannah** *vases and bowls were matt-glazed in dark-brown with cream and orange hand-painted swirled decoration.*

**Cascade**, *essentially modern in style, consisted of distinctive vases in strong bold shapes, which were highly-glazed in subtle blendings of mauve, blue, yellow and brown.*

**Denby Village** *was introduced in 1979. It was more of a hamlet than a village as only four out of the original six small houses, skilfully designed and modelled by Wendy Johnson, were ever put into production. Three inches high, they were exact replicas of picturesque old cottages and houses.*

Denby celebrated the royal wedding of Charles and Diana in 1981 with an excess of commemorative ware but gave little priority to the production of art pottery. The transfer prints which decorated some of the tableware designs were applied to gift ware. In 1983/4 the trees of Savoy, the sweet-peas of Dauphine, and the pretty florals of Romance and Memories decorated vases, bowls and table lamps alongside two new series of decorative ware.

**Bouquet** *glazed in beige, displayed freely hand-painted, multi-coloured leaves.*

**Fresco** *glazed in two shades of green, bore etched abstract leaf sprays.*

**Fern, Moss** and **Bracken** *were textured vases and bowls glazed in pale-green and white, dark-green and soft-brown.*

It was not until the advent of the designer Richard Eaton in 1986/7 that Denby was to produce a series of decorative ware that was individual in style and proclaimed the true Denby tradition.

# CHAPTER 11

# TRANSITION – THE COLOROLL EFFECT
## 1987 - 1989

The new Coloroll management descended on Denby – literally – by helicopter, and proceeded to 'rationalise' it with a vengeance.

Their takeover in 1987 involved yet another change of name, this time to the clumsy Coloroll Tableware Ltd., Denby Tableware Division. Fortunately, their ruthless re-appraisal of the Denby scene proved, in hindsight, to be its salvation. They restored both management and design functions to the site and set about weeding out those products that were not selling and were cluttering up the warehouses. They also drastically reduced the number of ranges that were on offer. Some of the more conservative members of the staff were horrified but this was to be a turning point in the factory's recovery. A capital investment programme was introduced which fed in a massive cash transfusion that restored the failing company. New kilns and other capital equipment were purchased and the administration was streamlined by the introduction of computerised technology.

Fred Cooper took early retirement and a new Managing Director, Frank Martin, energetically began to introduce the new Coloroll style of management.

## RICHARD EATON

As design functions had been restored to the Pottery a whole new team had to be recruited. Three designers were sought; one to specialise in shapes, another in patterns, and a third as an all-rounder. On the strength of his earlier work, Richard Eaton was invited to attend for interview. He indicated that he would be happy to work in any of the three roles but was surprised to find, when he arrived at Denby, that he was the only designer to have been appointed. This meant that he had to manage the whole design department and control its day-to-day work. He was given no time for advance planning or design development. Design consultants were commissioned by Coloroll. These 'experts' did not understand stoneware and they had Stoke-on-Trent attitudes to designs based on earthenware and fine china. It was Denby's misfortune that these were the people who were given the power to decide what should be produced.

However, the influence of Richard Eaton was soon to be reflected in the design policy of Denby as he had a clear vision of the direction in which the pottery should be developed. One of his first tasks was to recruit first-class artists to work with him. So Yin Ching, who made a considerable contribution during her comparatively brief period at Denby was appointed in 1988, as was Claire Bernard, who had left Denby during the Crown House years. Together, the new design team led by Richard Eaton began the task of creating contemporary tableware designs which maintained the distinctively Denby look.

## CLAIRE BERNARD

Claire Bernard was to be responsible for many of the innovative decorative effects created on the tableware of the 1990s. Although she had no formal art school training, Claire had drawn and painted for as long as she could remember. Indeed, she feels that formal training might have inhibited her vision. Her approach to design is radical and almost anarchic. Recognising no goal posts and using no rulers or preconceptions, Claire paints with ceramic decorating colours as she would with water colours, straight onto the pot. Working closely with Denby's technicians and modellers she has achieved spectacular results.

Richard Eaton, c.1988.

So Yin Ching, c.1988

Claire Bernard, 1997.

Denby Pottery

Left to right: Frank Martin, with John Ashcroft presenting the Chairman's Idea of the Year Award, 1988, to David Jeffrey, (far right) Stephen Riley.

Quickly tiring of her first job in a bank, Claire had originally joined Denby in 1979, working as a decorator with Glyn Colledge. Glyn recognised her talents and after a month she was promoted to the design studio, at first designing surface patterns for the shapes created by other designers. When Crown House took over the company in 1981 the designers' freedom was restricted. They were limited to five colours per design and expected to produce a new design every three months without the research and consideration that had previously ensured the traditional Denby quality. Eventually, the whole design team was made redundant and Claire left the company in 1986.

Rejecting the opportunity to work at the prestigious Wedgwood factory in Stoke-on-Trent, she became successful as a freelance artist, illustrating books, posters and calendars as well as selling her increasingly popular water colours, before returning to Denby.

In conjunction with the marketing department the design team conducted the research necessary to anticipate future customer demand, exploring current

fashion trends and discovering what was popular in Denby's European and American markets.

Between eight and twelve sample patterns would be presented to a group of experienced buyers whose opinions would be sought. Consumer research was conducted to examine current trends and to make informed predictions. Denby had found that there was a subtle difference between what customers said they liked and what they finally bought. A design had to be appropriate for all types of food – from breakfast cornflakes to the Sunday roast dinner.

This procedure was a far cry from the simple methods adopted by Joseph Bourne but was essential in the new international and technological age. Richard Eaton's research policy ensured that Denby was able to face the challenge of international competition in the 1990s.

## STEPHEN RILEY

In 1988 Coloroll appointed a new Managing Director, Stephen Riley, who had long experience of industry and the dynamic, yet down-to-earth approach that a revitalised Denby would need. His style of management was in complete contrast to that of John Ashcroft, the chairman of Coloroll in 1989.

John Ashcroft wrote in his 1989 annual report that he was pleased to say that the Group's profits had increased by one hundred percent. It was also recorded that his own salary had tripled to £517.000. Coloroll's takeover of Denby and other firms is described in the *Independent on Sunday* of 21st November 1993. The article relates how Coloroll insisted on putting its name above that of Denby on its products, a strategy that Stephen Riley is reported to have thought, 'seemed to break all the rules of marketing'. Coloroll also asked Denby to co-ordinate designs with those of the parent group but, 'fortunately we couldn't do it for technical reasons', recalled Stephen Riley. Generally speaking, however, the local Denby management was allowed a relatively free hand to revive the Pottery. In the same interview with the *Independent on Sunday*, Stephen Riley expressed the opinion that Denby did not fit in with Coloroll's image. By the October of 1989 he and his colleagues were considering a management buy-out.

# RETURN TO ORIGINS

In 1987 with Coloroll in firm control, tough and decisive policies axed many of the tableware designs which, viewed as a whole, lacked cohesion, style and identity. Cookware was given a new lease of life with the emphasis placed on current requirements of the modern household with ware designed specifically for use in a microwave oven.

Coloroll introduced one new contemporary-styled collection. The Artisan Collection was retained and the universal appeal of the shapes in the Sherwood Collection recognised. Although they continued to be decorated

successfully with floral patterns it was the application of typically Denby single-coloured glazes which transformed this Collection.

### The Seasons Cookware
**Orchard, Harvest** and **Autumn** *displayed seasonal fruits and vegetables in warm earth colours. Orchard, in terracotta brown, displayed a selection of apples, pears and grapes drawn by Thelma Hague whilst the seasonal Harvest vegetables and the blackberries, horse-chestnut leaves and conkers of the Autumn scene were beautifully illustrated by Claire Bernard.*

## THE COLLECTIONS

### The Discovery Collection

*The clean, square lines of the shapes designed by Rodney Endean indicated the direction in which Denby tableware was to develop. The basic shapes were presented in two completely different ways. Some relied on both glaze and surface pattern for their appeal, whilst others were simply glazed and differentiated by a band of moulded vertical lines:*

**Saturn** and **Chorus** were issued in 1987, with Saturn by Claire Bernard glazed in 'hares-fur' grey with narrow, widely spaced, dark vertical lines, and Chorus ridged and matt-glazed in a straw colour.

**Mercury, Kashmir** and **Autumn Gold** were introduced the following year. Mercury was a striking futuristic design in a rich, dark-green with diagonal, transfer printed swirled decoration. It was not designed 'in house'. The ridged Kashmir and Autumn Gold were glazed in mink-grey and white and in russet respectively.

### The Artisan Collection (second version)

*Coloroll continued to market the five designs that had been in production the previous year:*

**Decoy Duck**, a new pattern issued in 1987, primarily for the American market, was richly glazed in brown with cream, brown-rimmed plates encircled by ducks.

### The Sherwood Collection

*This was developed in two directions:*

**Images, Maplewood, Encore** and **Tasmin** *continued the floral theme with Images and Maplewood issued in 1987, Encore in 1988 and Tasmin by Claire Bernard, in 1989. Her patterns for Daybreak and Twilight were retained from the original series. Images, Maplewood and Encore had previously been marketed on other shapes as Memories, Sandalwood and Dauphine respectively. A competition was held for the re-naming of Thelma Hague's Dauphine. This was won by a team from the factory shop. As the pattern was to be a repeat their suggestion of Encore was judged to be the most appropriate.*

**Colonial Blue**, *followed by* **Imperial Blue** *and* **Regency Green** *represented the most significant change when, in 1988 and in 1989, Sherwood shapes were decorated in typical Denby glazes with white interiors. They followed in the  tradition of Cottage Blue and Manor Green with beautiful glazes which focused attention on natural shapes.*

# DECORATIVE WARE

# RICHARD EATON

Gradually the strong tradition of individually hand-decorated ware was phased out but not before the creation of Origins, a new range of decorative pottery in which the true Denby tradition was presented in the modern idiom. The highly individual contemporary styled vases, pitchers, bowls, lamp bases and planters were designed by Richard

Sgraffito artist decorating **Origins**, c.1986.

Eaton in 1986 whilst he was still a student gaining work experience at Denby and marketed by Coloroll the following year.

## ORIGINS

**Amber**, *highly-glazed in a glowing, speckled russet, showed off the distinguished shapes to perfection producing a dynamic effect reminiscent of the way in which Electric Blue enhanced Denby shapes in the 1920s.*

**Ebony** *was matt-glazed in ebony-brown which was cut through by precise sgraffito lines showing cream and arranged in triangular patterns.*

**Ivory** *was similarly decorated, as a direct response to the success of Ebony, but with the colours in reverse.*

**Suede** *planters in chestnut-brown displayed vertical sgraffito lines which exposed the light-coloured body.*

Sadly, after this high point of creativity and achievement, Denby ceased any significant production of decorative ware, with Richard Eaton's design skills directed towards creating decorative tableware, unique in style and quality.

To contrast with the light, floral pastels of much of the gift ware, two dark, highly-glossed series, with over-all patterns, were presented in the same year .

**Gemini** *vases and bowls were highly-glazed in deep olive-green enlivened by random pairs of small, ochre-coloured marks.*

**Eclipse** *lamp bases and toilet sets in deep-blue were decorated with a sponged pattern of small flecked squares in black and white.*

Vases and table lamps continued to be made to match existing tableware exactly or to harmonise with it.

# CHAPTER 12

# ON COURSE FOR THE TWENTY-FIRST CENTURY
# 1990 - 1997

Although Denby's owners, Coloroll, had appeared to be on the crest of a commercial wave in 1989 and its Chairman, John Ashcroft, was awarded the C.B.E., astute observers were noticing that it was in danger of overreaching itself. Coloroll had taken over the Crowther Carpet Group in an increasingly difficult trading environment and, by June 1990, was in receivership.

Aware of the Group's problems during 1989, members of the Denby Board of Management had been tempted to consider a management buy-out and made tentative, informal approaches to ostensibly friendly members of the Coloroll Board. The response was decidedly hostile with threats of dismissal if preparations for a buy-out proceeded. Although the project appeared to have been extinguished, to quote Denby's report of the buy-out, 'the flame of

Stephen Riley.

independence had been ignited' and was 'almost impossible to douse'. As Coloroll's problems worsened, several of its other subsidiaries also began to consider a management buy-out as a contingency measure. Eventually, no less than seven of them took this action.

When the receivers were finally called in on 7th June, the Denby Board was free to make its bid for a buy-out and immediately consulted contacts in Aynsley China who had successfully staged a buy-out from the Wedgwood Group of Potteries. Their advice was invaluable. Experienced specialist solicitors were engaged and the workforce and media were informed of the Board's plans.

Unfortunately, the Receiver was compelled to offer the company to any suitable buyer and over one hundred and eighty requests for information about Denby Pottery were received. This placed the Board in the schizophrenic position of, on the one hand, having to assist the Receiver to sell the business to prospective buyers and, at the same time, to make presentations on their own behalf to prospective venture capitalists in order to raise the funds they would need to buy-out the Company.

Six five-hour presentations including a full factory tour, were made to representatives of these financial institutions who seemed to be more interested in the company's assets rather than its growth, profit-record and potential. At the same time, the Denby management team had to co-operate fully with the Receiver and be 'paraded in front of potential rival purchasers'. It was a time of great strain and nerves were stretched to the uttermost. There was continuous debate within the team as to how much to offer and what tactics to adopt, but members kept their nerve and solidarity.

By the fifth week of receivership the increasingly confident Denby team chose the '3i' Group to support its buy-out bid. There were, nevertheless, many anxious moments as the Receiver continued to prevaricate and other companies threatened last minute bids. Eventually the Receiver agreed to consider Denby's offer and intensive nerve-racking negotiations commenced.

Denby's report describes how the management team wandered around the London offices of the Receiver's lawyers 'trying not to get in the way', whilst the lawyers and accountants and advisers hammered out a deal. Negotiations went on throughout the night of the 22nd July 1990. Towards midnight a consensus emerged and by 3 am no less than twenty-three people were involved in working on the agreement. Eventually, to the Denby team's intense relief, a new business emerged at precisely 4.27 am on the morning of 23rd July. As the sun rose over the river Thames, the team celebrated with champagne before heading back to Denby.

The strength and unity of the buy-out team, the quality of its advisers, and 'one hell of a lot of luck' had enabled Denby to regain its independence. As members of the Denby team had invested much of their own personal capital into the buy-out, the celebrations must have been tinged with a certain amount of trepidation as the vista of independence stretched out before them.

The new Management Board was relieved to find that their confidence in the Pottery was justified. Following the success of the management buy-out and despite a deepening depression, customer demand for Denby stoneware has remained undiminished. By 1994 the thriving company was successfully floated on the stock exchange.

## DENBY TODAY

Key figures in management and design have punctuated Denby's progress throughout two centuries. Today, Denby Pottery, led by its Group Chief Executive, Stephen Riley, emphasises the team approach and relies on an informal but positive management style based on consultation, delegation, research and strict product control. The new management team, adapting to global business practices, has a clear vision of Denby in the 1990s whilst Richard Eaton the Design Director, ensures that the true Denby style is preserved by developing and maintaining the tradition of quality, characteristic glazes and original designs.

A significant change in contemporary life-style has led to increasing demands for casual tableware that is of good quality, modern in style and practical to use. With the improvement in communications generally, the design, marketing and sales departments are responding to international influences and markets. Denby is one of the few potteries that is successful in retaining its own individual identity whilst adapting to current trends. It is unique in today's market. As Stephen Riley quotes, 'The harder you practice, the luckier you get'. Denby has been practising for almost two hundred years.

The development and increasingly high profile of the Denby Visitors Centre is a direct response to a change in shopping patterns. Paradoxically, the past is becoming a living part of Denby as visitors to the Factory Shop view the Museum and recognise the links between the pottery which they are buying for their own table and that created by Denby craftspeople almost two hundred years ago. Tableware of the 1950s and 1960s is already proving to be a rich and varied source for collectors and similarly the striking designs of the 1990s are poised to become the collectables of the twenty-first century.

It is typical that people managing a pottery tend to become so involved with day-to-day activities that all attention becomes focused on the next product. Fortunately, as company policy, many records and old pieces of pottery have been collected and preserved, in the first instance by Eileen White and currently by Linda Salt.

Linda Salt.

In 1987 Glyn Colledge and a local ceramics historian, Richard Hughes, commenced cataloguing the extensive collection which Linda continued on taking over the museum in the same year.

No member of the Denby team is more committed than Linda, whose grandmother was making **Penny Duds** at the beginning of this century. Linda is not only Curator of the Museum but also the Public Relations Officer for the company, and Personal Assistant to the Group Chief Executive. An acknowledged expert on early Denby pottery she is constantly asked to date and name old pieces which are brought to the Museum for identification. Indeed, she has even been known to assist the current design team by suggesting names for the next year's designs. At Denby Pottery the old and the new are inextricably linked.

Without a Bourne or a Wood or a Dale or a Colledge, but with the accumulated expertise of two centuries of talented designers and a skilled and loyal workforce, the Denby management team has restored the Pottery's fortunes. The true spirit of Denby has been revived and flourishes today.

# ARTISTRY WITH TECHNOLOGY

It was actually Denby tableware of the nineties which stimulated the authors to research Denby pottery. On a cold November day in 1993 the sight of Shiraz, Marrakesh and Baroque brilliantly lit and massed together in the local Debenhams was a revelation. It was not just the colour, or the shapes, or the patterns, but the whole concept of the design which generated an element of excitement. What was surprising was that when the discovery was mentioned to friends and colleagues with a shared interest in ceramics, they too had noted and recognised the quality of these new designs. It felt 'right', it was the pottery for the 1990s.

Nostalgia and innovation were combined in kitchen ware.

## Classic and Chef Cookware
*Traditional brown, green and blue-glazed cookware, reminiscent of the 1930s, was re-introduced in 1990 for a short period before the contemporary glazes of Chef Ware took precedence.*

## The Seasons Cookware

**Winter,** *a new scene in pristine white evoked a crisp frosty morning with a distant farmhouse framed by the dried stems of meadow-sweet, mushrooms, bracken and highlighted by brilliant red berries. It was finely drawn by Claire Bernard.*

The Discovery range was withdrawn and the production of decorative art pottery had virtually ceased. The design department now flourished under the leadership of Richard Eaton. His original tableware designs, entirely appropriate for Denby clay, were absolutely right for the contemporary scene and together with the inspirational decorative effects conjured by Claire Bernard they formed a significant part of the ongoing pageant that is Denby pottery.

## TABLEWARE

### The Columbia Series
*Launched in 1990, the distinctive shapes by Richard Eaton, featuring a curved contour line, were extremely popular on the continent, especially in Germany. Some were highly-glazed in sophisticated colours, others were transfer-printed with a floral design by Claire Bernard:*

**Parisienne** and **Saville Grey** *were glazed in olive-green and dark-grey respectively.*

**Tivoli** and **Mandarin** *displayed pastel flowers which echoed the contour line and the shape of the ware. Tivoli was garlanded and Mandarin, introduced in 1991, illustrated a powder-blue convolvulus.*

**The Artisan Collection** (second version)
*Camelot and Pampas were soon phased out. Two contrasting designs, Greystone with its plain earth glazes, and the more sophisticated Midnight, were retained until the mid-1990s.*

**The Sherwood Collection**
*Although Images was discontinued in 1993, Tasmin, Daybreak, Encore and Damask remained in production until the mid-1990s as did Colonial Blue, Imperial Blue and Regency Green. Gradually classic glazes were replacing the floral patterns:*

**Damask,** *issued in 1991, exhibited full-blown flowers drawn by Claire Bernard onto a deep, salmon-pink ground.*

**Viceroy,** *in the same year, extended the range of colours with a new light brown glaze.*

## THE SOVEREIGN SHAPE

*Good as previous tableware designs had been, it was the Sovereign Shapes of 1992, with their imaginative decoration, which won so much acclaim. The shapes were designed by Richard Eaton and he controlled the whole project. When the team was considering names for the new shapes, Sovereign was considered an appropriate choice as the four panels of the tea and coffee pots were said to represent the four decades of Queen Elizabeth's reign which was about to be celebrated.*

*This elegant tableware was dominated by an archetypal teapot or coffee pot. Perfectly balanced, the lid, spout and handle formed part of a harmonious whole. Richly-glazed on the exterior, the interior of cups, jugs, bowls and the centres of plates were glazed in a clear white. The innovative decorative effects were created mainly by Claire Bernard who approached her work as an artist and an iconoclast:*

**Marrakesh** *was unusually glazed in a lightly-textured shade of dark sand, highlighted by strips of jewel-like mosaic. The decoration had gradually emerged from an idea Claire had been developing for ten years. The source of her inspiration was a small, round box decorated in the mosaic style. Indeed, before Marrakesh was put on the market, the design team had always referred to it as 'Mosaic'.*

**Baroque** *was glazed in rich mid-blue featuring an art nouveau style pendant which glowed in a medley of subtle blues, turquoise, pink, and orange. It was drawn entirely freehand by Claire Bernard and had a vitality and 'element of uncertainty' that could not have been achieved if it had been drawn with mechanical precision.*

**Shiraz**, *issued in 1993, was developed by So Yin Ching. It was distinguished by a most sophisticated colourway in which diamond-patterned bands in red, purple, blue, and yellow were set against a lustrous, plum-coloured ground. The large service platter decorated entirely in diamonds created a three dimensional 'Op Art' illusion. Quite spectacular, it is predicted that it will become a collector's item.*

**Regatta**, *glazed alternately in royal blue and green, emphasised the shapes to good effect.*

Of the four designs, only Shiraz has been discontinued.

## THE MERIDIAN SHAPE

*A new set of shapes was created in which So Yin Ching played a major role. The sophisticated green and blue glazes were the modern equivalent of the art glazes of the 1920s:*

**Greenwich** *was glazed in deep sea-green with white contrast. First issued in 1994, its excellence was rewarded the following year when the Gift Ware Association of Great Britain voted it the Tableware Gift of The Year.*

**Luxor** *co-ordinated in turquoise-green, cream and ivory, echoed both in colour and decoration, the artistry of ancient Egypt. A contrasting, dentulated band, highlighted by jewel-like colours transformed each piece, and the effect created varied according to the shape of the surface to which the design was applied. The large decorative platter was a contemporary masterpiece of the potter's art. Produced in 1995, this Denby classic, elegant in its simplicity, was achieved by a combination of the highest artistic and the latest technological skills. Luxor was selected Tableware Gift of the Year in 1996.*

**Boston** *was glazed in denim blue with cream contrast in 1995.*

**Boston Spa**, *introduced in 1997, was a decorative variation of Boston. Inspired by Byzantine mosaics, the precise, geometric pattern, in deep sea-green, purple, amber, and ivory, was applied using the same unique litho technique previously employed on Luxor. The sunburst effect on the large platter created a memorable image.*

The high reputation of Denby pottery is now represented by the unique quality and style of its decorative tableware. A major new tableware shape is created every three or four years and at least one new surface pattern is originated each year. The epitome of good design, its decorative qualities are equalled by its practicality and by its fitness for purpose. It is pottery for today and for the future.

## CASUAL TABLEWARE

The public's imagination was caught by the ingenious development of two series of colour co-ordinated cookware and tableware by Richard Eaton. Available in three plain colours, each piece was glazed in at least two out of three colours. The effect was simultaneously diverse and unified:

**The Harlequin Series** *in dark shades of crimson, blue, and turquoise-green was first issued in 1992.*

**The Spice Series** *in yellow, green, and brown followed the next year.*

**Metz**, *dominated by a rich vibrant blue glaze was highlighted by a green, almost luminous, rim. Two variations of a magnificent platter, diamond-checked in blue, green, and white, were co-ordinated with white or green plates banded in blue, rimmed in green. Metz was designed by Sarah Heaton in 1996.*

### Mugs

Mugs were produced in profusion. Claire Bernard told the authors that compared to the development of a tableware series, 'A mug project is like a day at the seaside – relaxing. Ideas may be developed into a series of either tableware or cookware. Mugs are a way of testing the water.' She designed the Flame and the Batik mugs.

# DESIGN MISCELLANY

## GLYN ON GLYN WARE

'Glyn Ware was made to create post-war prestige, give us training but, most importantly, was to avoid the purchase tax of the time. Every piece was decorated to a theme, sprays, leaves, but no flowers, no two alike. Fruit bowls, beer mugs, cider sets, nut bowls, goblets, lemonade jugs etc.

When bone-dry a white slip (liquid clay) was sprayed on and the pieces were then fired in a pre-war tunnel kiln to make the pots vitreous. They were then taken to the 'girls' who put on backgrounds, bands and decoration – non-floral, with Byzantine, Italian and Persian classic design influences. Girls learning to paint always had to take home their first respectable piece. Underglaze colours were all 'dirtied' to take away the crudeness of Stoke suppliers' colours – old gold, sage, mushroom, knicker blue, duck muck, banana sick, all names to stick in trainees' minds.

The decorated ware was taken to be sprayed in transparent glaze if the motif was to be clear like hunting scenes or coaching scenes, but the majority were the 'leafy' patterns glazed in the semi-matt glaze which brought out the wonderful blue of the copper oxide, the vivid yellow-green of chrome oxide and the vibrant plum colour of manganese dioxide. The ware was then re-fired at a lower temperature in the same tunnel kiln, both fires having taken around sixteen hours each. They were sprayed in batches by one good girl, because of lack of porosity and thinness of application, wiped and fired again in the tunnel kiln not at 1225 degrees centigrade but at 1050 degrees...

The Glyn Ware was a good training for the more profitable and large orders of tableware which was to follow. Hand-painted tableware caught on quickly all over the world, but the one which put Denby on the map was Greenwheat. The change from Glyn Ware to decorating on fired plates, casseroles, cups etc. was quite rapid and teams were formed and one girl did a portion or segment of the set pattern very rapidly.'

## GLYN ON GLYNBOURNE

'The textured Glynbourne was a good seller over a period of years and consisted of bowls, big ashtrays, jugs and vases. Giftware lines were always once-fired for economy, so in this case they were coated with a white glaze on the clay as a batch, then the pressure turned down and a stiffer and gummed white glaze spattered to give the surface. I remember the tall, narrow-necked vase took me two hours to do nicely. The 'Time Study Bods' were giving twenty minutes to girls to make a bonus. Some gift ware lines lasted longer in time than others but there was always one on the go, to give the reps a change and seaside gift shops a choice.'

## RICHARD EATON

### Design Philosophy
In August 1995, Richard Eaton, currently Design Director at Denby, summarised his design philosophy as follows:

'I believe that in today's market a ceramic designer has to wear many hats. It is not only the ability to design an appealing pattern or an interesting shape concept. A designer has to have a broad knowledge of what is happening in the ever-changing world of interior design and home fashion and this can only be done by researching and spending time in the world's markets.

As designers we are always endeavouring to create impactive and distinctive designs, that are at the leading edge of popular taste.

It is the designers brief to bring together his knowledge of the market as well as production processes in order to develop cost effective designs that often push production technology and skills to the limits. This can only be done by working as a team with every area in the business from Technical and Production through to Sales and Marketing.

A designer can no longer work in an ivory tower.'

### From the potters wheel to the computer
In keeping with this philosophy, Richard has realised that a designer in the 1990s must use modern technology to assist him or her. Explaining how he came to use Computer Aided Design, he tells us:

'The Design Department encompasses four designers and two technicians with a modeller and an in-house print department also at its disposal. All the shapes, patterns and glazes are completely designed in-house and in many respects the design process is very much like that of a small art pottery. In fact Denby could at times be classed as a very large Studio Pottery and as such has had a number of world renowned potters working in its studio. Today, because of the processes used and the amount of engineering that goes into the production of modern ceramic tableware, the skills required in our design team range from industrial design through to being a skilled hand-painter.

The production processes used at Denby range from ram pressing, jollying and casting through to hand-throwing and the patterns are applied by decal. These are all aspects of manufacturing that a designer obviously has to be fully aware of when designing any new design for shape or pattern.

Although we work with coloured glazes and reactive colours all the time we still find the only way to successfully design a pattern is by hand-painting straight on to the pottery and firing the pattern in order to see the results the kiln firing will give, in other words, designing by experimentation and trial and error, the way that Denby designers have developed patterns for over a century.

Shape design has always been very important to Denby as it is our belief that it is the combination of good shape with the right interesting glaze colour and pattern that goes towards the making of a winning design. If one of these factors is wrong the overall design will fall down. Like pattern and glaze development, shapes are always under review whether it be the change of something small and simple like an egg cup, the development of a new mug shape or even a complete dinnerware range.

A new tableware range might only be launched every three or four years but in between those times there are often numerous changes to be made to existing shapes that often go unnoticed but take a great deal of design and development time. Shape concepts for potential new ranges will also be at various stages of development.

Certain aspects of shape design have remained unchanged. We still work to a design brief, we still research design trends and styles etc. and we still start a project by sketching a number of ideas on paper, but after this, the design process has moved from the drawing board onto the computer.

I first started to research the world of Computer Aided Design three years ago, partially out of an interest in knowing what was available in this unfamiliar world and partially knowing that as Denby invested in new computer assisted machinery, more accurate drawings and data would be required from the designer to produce the tools needed. The only way I knew we could provide such information would be through the use of computer software. It was this thinking, along with the knowledge that new shapes are continuously being developed and the design process needed to be accelerated that moved me into using computer technology.

...I decided on a number of principles that the system had to fulfil. Firstly the software had to fit in with the way we worked in the Design Department and had to be simple enough to create the shapes required...I eventually came across a package that was just coming out of its development stages...it answered all the issues I had outlined...

Denby became the first company in the U.K. to install this system into its design studio in December 1992 and after only two days of training we were designing the next shape range to be launched. (The system) gives us the power we need to manipulate and view three dimensional models...it also gives us the ability to move into Computer Aided Machining at a later date...

The item being designed is built from two-dimensional curves in very much the same way as designing on paper. It is very quick and easy to create complex surfaces which can be edited and immediately visualised as a three-dimensional model...the software

has given the designer more time to experiment and explore different alternative shape ideas which would have been difficult on paper...

The software can also give the physical properties of a model...it is easy to produce a high quality image of the finished model.

Having a computer aided design system in the studio has not radically changed the overall way that we design, we still use whatever the best tool is for the job in question, whether it be hand-painting a pot to see a glaze effect or throwing a pot on the potter's wheel through to sketching ideas and developing them through computer assisted design, any process or tool is at the disposal of the design department to create a new design in shape, colour and pattern.

The benefits of using a computer has certainly enabled us to develop and review more designs both quickly and with more conviction as it is now possible, and easier, to make earlier design decisions that will affect a design's development.

Now we have the ability to show a three-dimensional object either on the screen or on paper it is easier to present new ideas for product development whether it be internally or to a potential customer...'.

The technique described by Richard Eaton is a far cry from that used by earlier designers such as Horace Elliot, Kenneth Clark or even Glyn Colledge. They would visualise a shape or design, then reproduce it in a pattern book or directly onto the clay. The computer designer can now transfer his or her ideas onto the 'virtual reality' of a computer screen before committing them to paper or clay. Nevertheless, as Richard implies, the basic principle remains – the designer must first have the vision which can be translated to pottery using one of several tools, including the computer.

When Glyn Colledge visited the modern design studio in 1995 the computer aided design was demonstrated to him and he readily acknowledged its value but, as he and Richard Eaton would agree, the vision must come first and the computer is just another sophisticated tool.

Apart from the technology, it is the status of the designer that has changed over the centuries. At first, he or she was regarded as merely another operative and was paid accordingly. Eventually, progressive manufacturers such as Denby, realised the value of employing the most skilled and imaginative designers. At all times the designer has been a key figure in the success of a factory.

# DECORATIVE WARE SHAPES

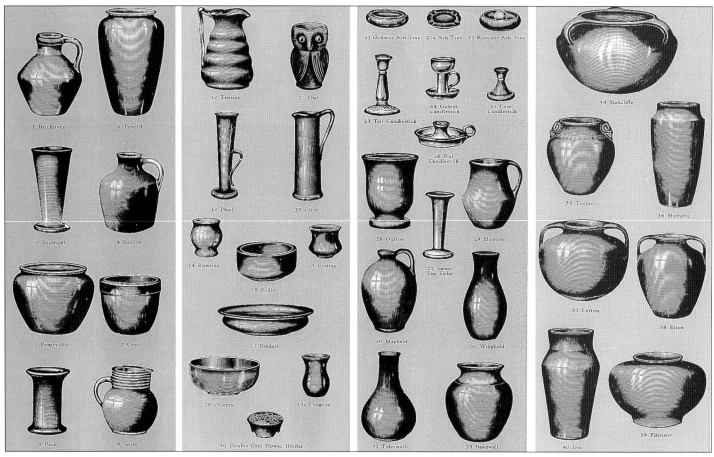

1 Birchover
2 Peveril
3 Trumpet
4 Baslow
5 Pembroke
7 Oriel
8 Park
9 Swiss

10 Tansley
11 Owl
12 Phial
13 Crich
14 Rowsley
15 Grattan
16 Sicilian
17 Eskdale
18 Oriental
19a Longnor
20 Double Grid Flower Holder

21 Godwin Ash Tray
21a Ash Tray
22 Knocker Ash Tray
23 Tall Candlestick
24 Goblet Candlestick
25 Low Candlestick
26 Flat Candlestick
28 Oulton
27 Sweet Pea Tube
29 Hopton
30 Mayfield
31 Wingfield
32 Tideswell
33 Bakewell

34 Stancliffe
35 Torino
36 Homeric
37 Lytton
38 Elton
39 Edensor
40 Iris

**Electric Blue**, c.1925.

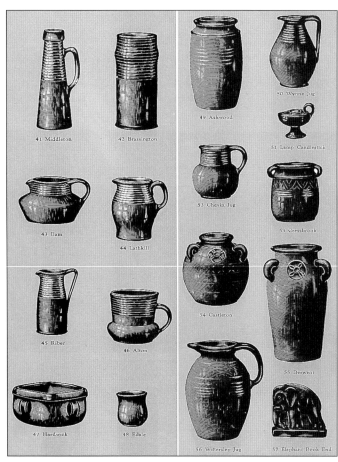

41 Middleton
42 Brassington
43 Ilam
44 Lathkill
45 Riber
46 Alton
47 Hardwick
48 Edale
49 Ashwood
50 Wynne Jug
51 Lamp Candlestick
52 Chevin Jug
53 Cressbrook
54 Castleton
55 Derwent
56 Willersley Jug
57 Elephant Book End

**Electric Blue**, c.1925.

No. 809 Chinley
No. 810 Sdacon
No. 811 Stretton
No. 801 Brailsford
No. 812 Milford
No. 802 Mackworth
No. 813 Duffield
No. 814 Heath
No. 803 Matlock
No. 804 Hainstead
No. 815 Belper
No. 805 Fairfield
No. 806 Hassop
No. 816 Book End
No. 817 Dethick
No. 807 Parwich
No. 808 Lumley

**Antique Green**, c.1930.

Orient Ware, c.1926.

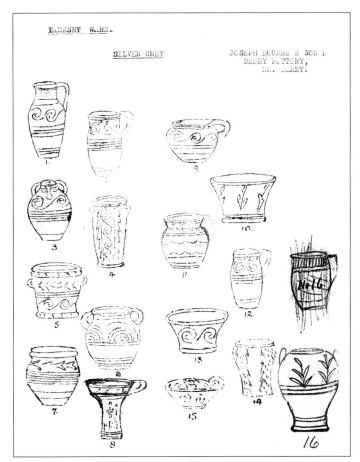

Silver Grey, c.1931.

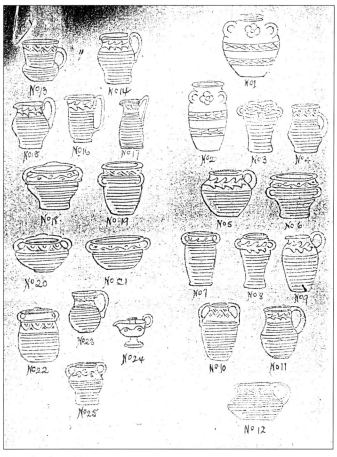

Moorland, c.1931.

Denby Pottery

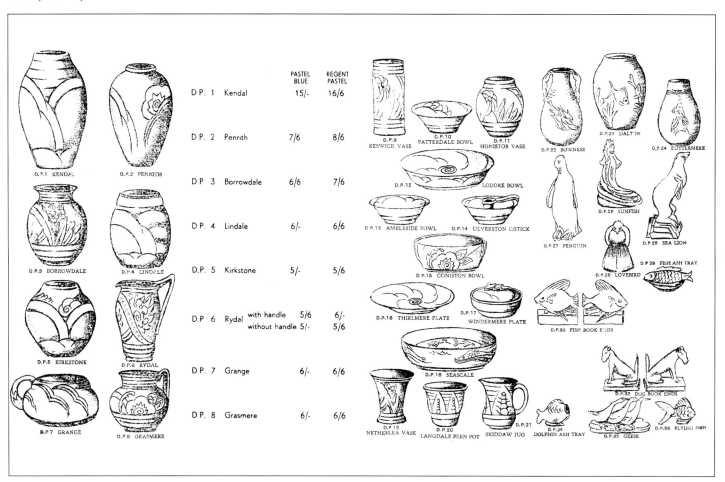

| | | | PASTEL BLUE | REGENT PASTEL |
|---|---|---|---|---|
| D P. 1 | Kendal | | 15/- | 16/6 |
| D P. 2 | Penrith | | 7/6 | 8/6 |
| D P. 3 | Borrowdale | | 6/6 | 7/6 |
| D P. 4 | Lindale | | 6/- | 6/6 |
| D P. 5 | Kirkstone | | 5/- | 5/6 |
| D P. 6 | Rydal | with handle | 5/6 | 6/- |
| | | without handle | 5/- | 5/6 |
| D P. 7 | Grange | | 6/- | 6/6 |
| D P. 8 | Grasmere | | 6/- | 6/6 |

**Danesby Pastel,** c.1933.

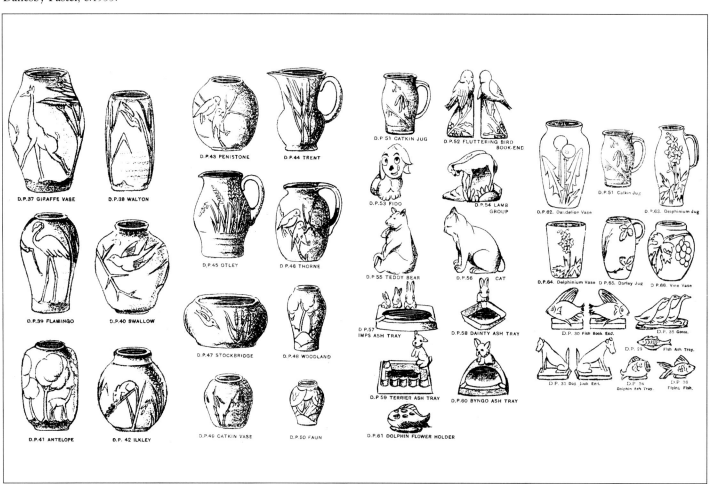

**Danesby Pastel,** c.1933.

**Sylvan Pastel,** c.1935.

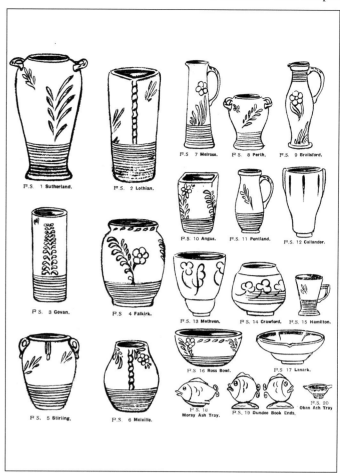

**Featherstone,** c.1936.

Garden Ware, c.1934.

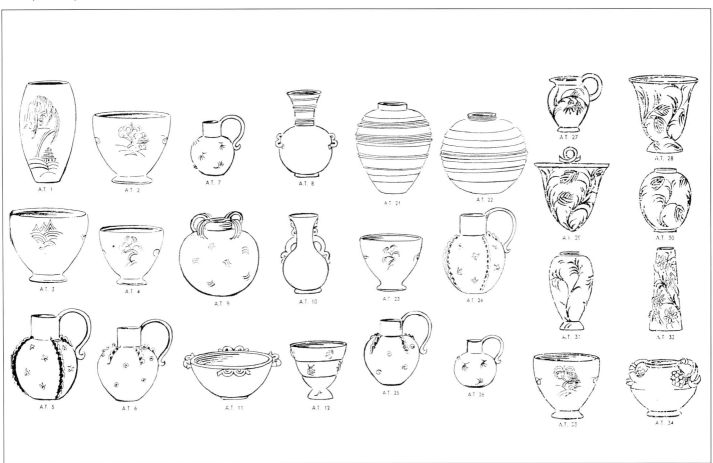

**Tyrolean Ware**, c.1937.

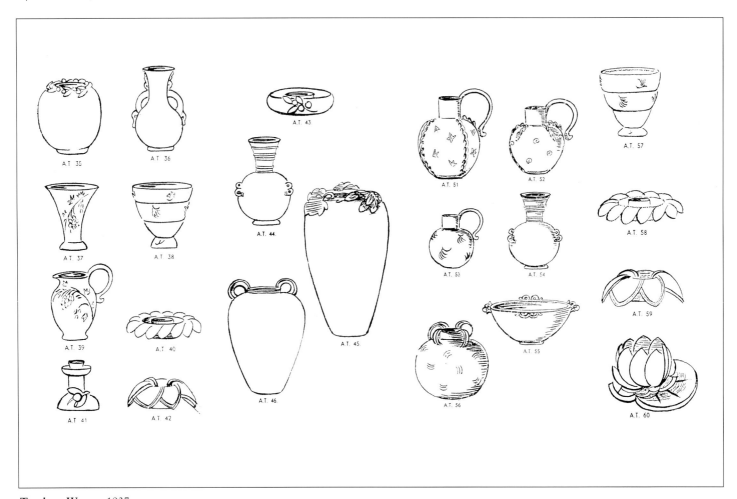

**Tyrolean Ware**, c.1937.

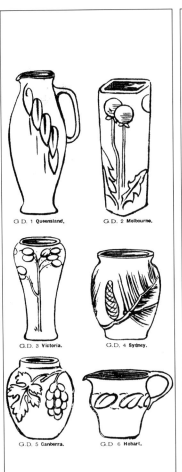

G.D. 1 Queensland.  G.D. 2 Melbourne.

G.D. 3 Victoria.  G.D. 4 Sydney.

G.D. 5 Canberra.  G.D 6 Hobart.

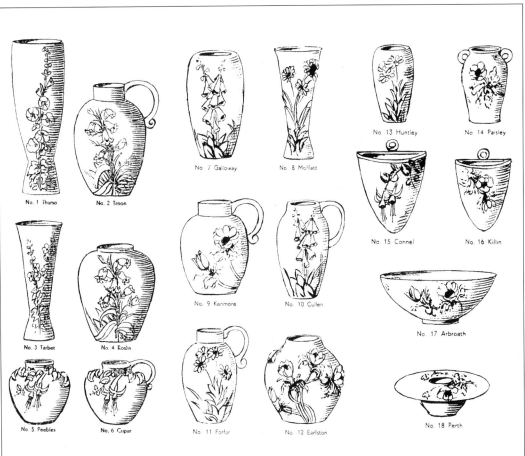

No. 1 Thurso  No. 2 Troon

No. 7 Galloway  No. 8 Moffatt

No 13 Huntley  No 14 Paisley

No. 3 Tarbet  No. 4 Roslin

No. 9 Kenmore  No. 10 Cullen

No. 15 Connel  No. 16 Killin

No. 5 Peebles  No. 6 Cupar

No. 11 Forfar  No. 12 Earlston

No. 17 Arbroath

No. 18 Perth

**Floral Pastel**, c.1937/8.

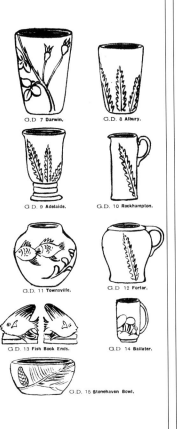

G.D. 7 Darwin.  G.D. 8 Albury.

G.D. 9 Adelaide.  G.D. 10 Rockhampton.

G.D. 11 Townsville.  G.D 12 Forfar.

G.D. 13 Fish Book Ends.  G.D 14 Bailater.

G.D. 15 Stonehaven Bowl.

No. 1.

No. 2.

No. 5.

No. 9.

No. 6.

No. 10.

No. 11.

No. 3.

No. 4.

No. 7.

No. 8.

No. 12.

No. 13.

**Greenland**, c.1936/7.  **Folkweave**, c.1938/9.

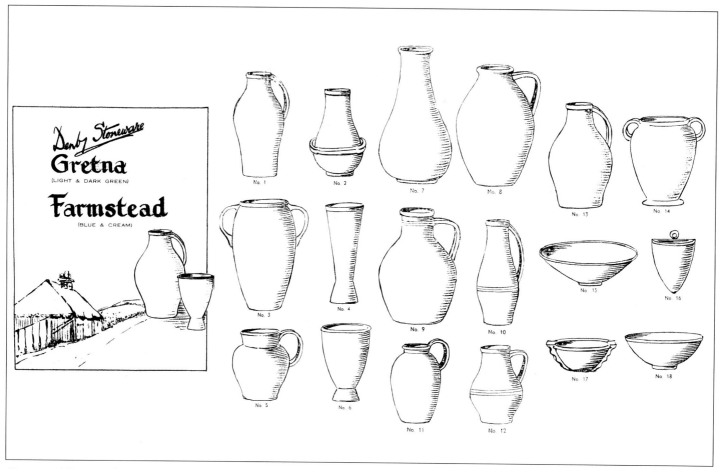

**Gretna** and **Farmstead**, c.1937/8

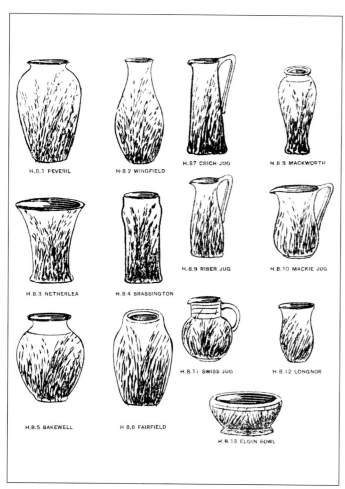

**Herbaceous Border,** mid-to late-1930s.

**Ivory Pastel,** late-1930s.

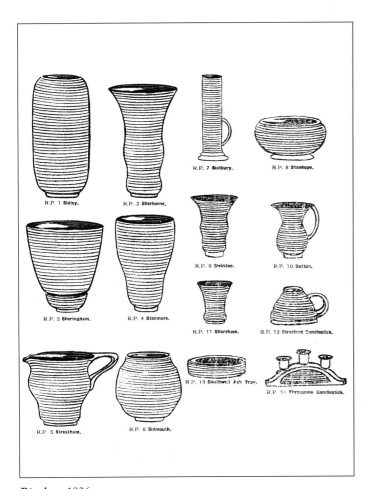

**Ripple,** c.1936.

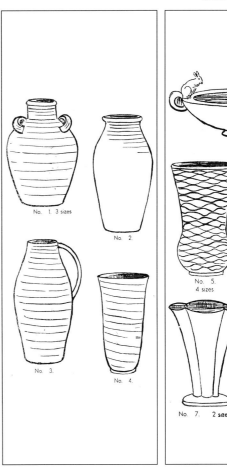

**Old Ivory** (part), c.1939.

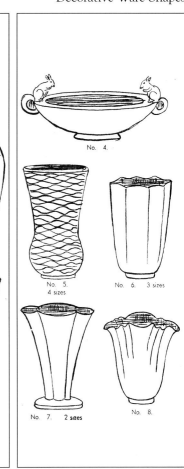

**Waverley** (part), c.1939.

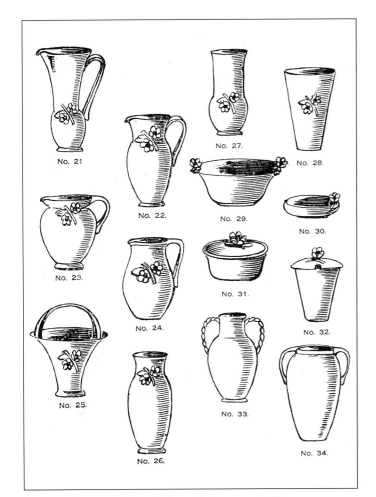

**Old English, Spring Time, Tibet** and **Cottage,** c.1939.

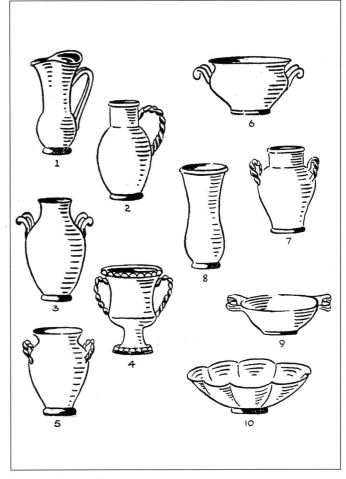

**Gay Border,** c.1948.

Denby Pottery

Animals, c.1930s.

124

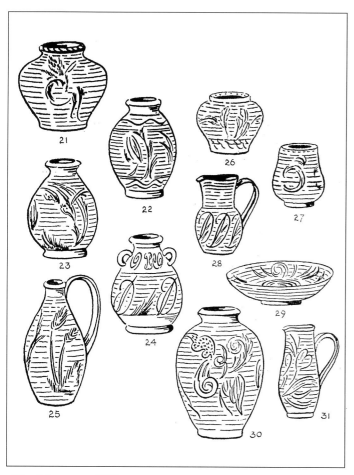

**Glyndebourne**, c.1948.

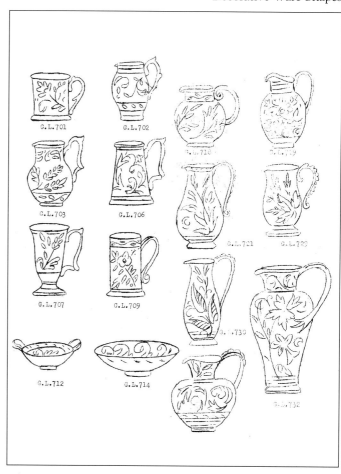

**Glyn Ware**, c.1950.

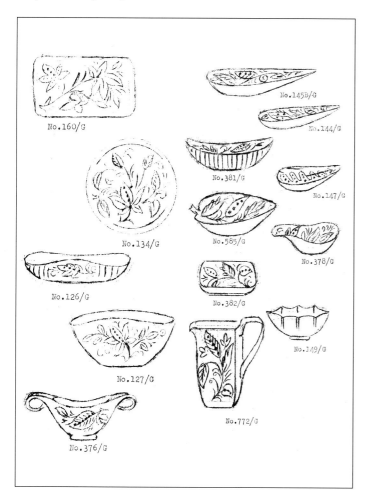

**New Glyn Ware**, mid-1950s.

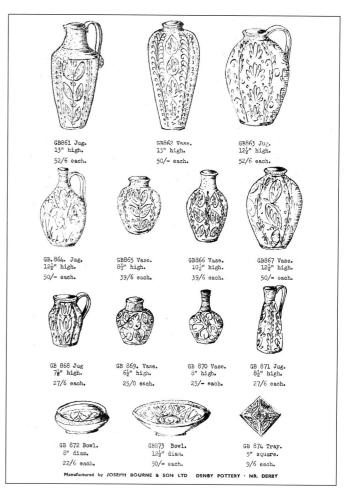

**Glynbourne**, c.1960.

# CHEVIOT

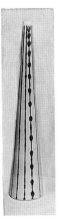     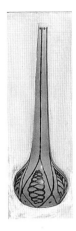 

| CH 501 | CH 502 | CH 503 | CH 504 | CH 505 | CH 506 | CH 507 |
|---|---|---|---|---|---|---|
| 19″ high | 16¼″ **high** | 17¼″ high | 12″ high | 163? high | 18? high | 173? high |

CH 501. CH 502    Black with etched decoration ⎫
CH 503. CH 506    Grey with etched decoration ⎬ 5 . 5 . 0
CH 505                   Litchen green with etched ⎭   each
                              decoration
CH 504                   White only . . . . . 3.3.0 each
CH 501. CH 502. CH 503. CH 505. CH 506. CH 507
                   in White . . 3.15.0 each

CH 503    Blue with black decoration ⎫
CH 501    Yellow with black decoration ⎬
CH 502    Green with white decoration ⎪ 4 . 10 . 0
CH 507    Red with white decoration ⎪   each
CH 506    Purple with black decoration ⎭

**CH 508    BOWL**
Black with etched decoration
11″ x 6¾″ high          85/- each

**CH 520    BOWL**
Purple with black decoration
9″ x 3¼″ high          42/6 each

**CH 509    TRAY**
Black with etched decoration
8¼″ x 3½″  . . .    17/6 each

**CH 521    BOWL**
Yellow with black
decoration
11½″ x 4½″ high    75/- each

**CH 510    DISH**
Grey with etched decoration
13¼″ x 3¼″ high    85/- each
8″ x 3¾″ high    35/- each

**CH 522    BOWL**
Green with white decoration
13″ long  . . .    75/- each

**CH 511    BOWL**
Black with etched decoration
6¼″ x 4″ high          39/6 each

**CH 512    PLATTER**
Green with etched decoration
12″ x 8″   . . .    67/- each
8″ x 8″   . . .    34/6 each

**Cheviot, mid-1950s.**

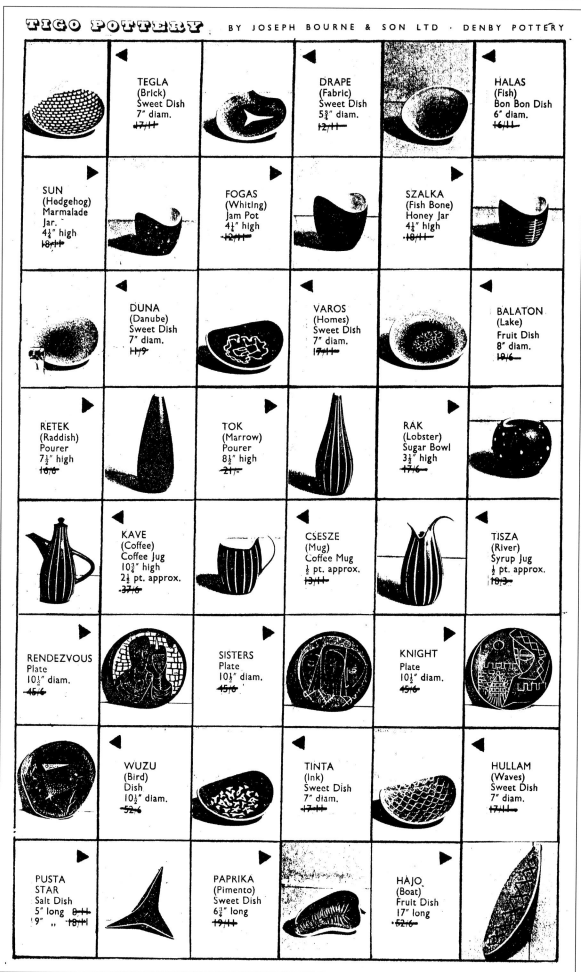

## TIGO POTTERY  BY JOSEPH BOURNE & SON LTD · DENBY POTTERY

TEGLA
(Brick)
Sweet Dish
7" diam.
17/11

DRAPE
(Fabric)
Sweet Dish
5¾" diam.
12/11

HALAS
(Fish)
Bon Bon Dish
6" diam.
16/11

SUN
(Hedgehog)
Marmalade
Jar.
4¼" high
18/11

FOGAS
(Whiting)
Jam Pot
4¼" high
12/11

SZALKA
(Fish Bone)
Honey Jar
4¼" high
18/11

DUNA
(Danube)
Sweet Dish
7" diam.
11/9

VAROS
(Homes)
Sweet Dish
7" diam.
17/11

BALATON
(Lake)
Fruit Dish
8" diam.
19/6

RETEK
(Raddish)
Pourer
7½" high
16/6

TOK
(Marrow)
Pourer
8½" high
21/-

RAK
(Lobster)
Sugar Bowl
3½" high
17/6

KAVE
(Coffee)
Coffee Jug
10¾" high
2½ pt. approx.
37/6

CSESZE
(Mug)
Coffee Mug
½ pt. approx.
13/11

TISZA
(River)
Syrup Jug
½ pt. approx.
18/3

RENDEZVOUS
Plate
10½" diam.
45/6

SISTERS
Plate
10½" diam.
45/6

KNIGHT
Plate
10½" diam.
45/6

WUZU
(Bird)
Dish
10½" diam.
52/6

TINTA
(Ink)
Sweet Dish
7" diam.
17/11

HULLAM
(Waves)
Sweet Dish
7" diam.
17/11

PUSTA
STAR
Salt Dish
5" long  8/11
9"  ,,  18/11

PAPRIKA
(Pimento)
Sweet Dish
6¼" long
19/11

HAJO
(Boat)
Fruit Dish
17" long
52/6

**Tigo Ware**, mid-1950s.

# COTSWOLD
designed by KENNETH CLARK

**JOSEPH BOURNE & SON LTD**
**DENBY POTTERY · Nr. DERBY**

| C.D.811 | C.D.812 | C.D.813 | C.D.814 |
|---|---|---|---|
| **WINDRUSH VASE** | **BIRDLIP JUG** | **STOWE VASE** | **BROADWAY PLANT POT** |
| 3½″ high 5/3 each | 6″ high 10/6 each | 4″ high 5/11 each | 3¾″ high 6/11 each |
| 4½″ high 7/6 each | 8″ high 13/11 each | 6″ high 8/6 each | 4¾″ high 9/11 each |
| 6″ high 11/6 each | 10″ high 18/6 each | 8″ high 12/6 each | 6″ high 12/11 each |
| 8½″ high 15/6 each | 12″ high 23/6 each | 10″ high 16/6 each | 8″ high 17/6 each |

| C.D.817. BIBURY FOOTED BOWL | C.D.815. BURFORD BOWL | C.D.818. PAINSWICK STEM VASE | C.D.816. CHEDWORTH BOWL |
|---|---|---|---|
| 5¼″ high 15/6 each | 7″ diam. 11/6 each | 6½″ high 15/6 each | 5¼″ diam. 10/6 each |
|  | 8″ diam. 14/11 each |  | 7″ diam. 14/6 each |

**Cotswold** (first version), mid-1950s.

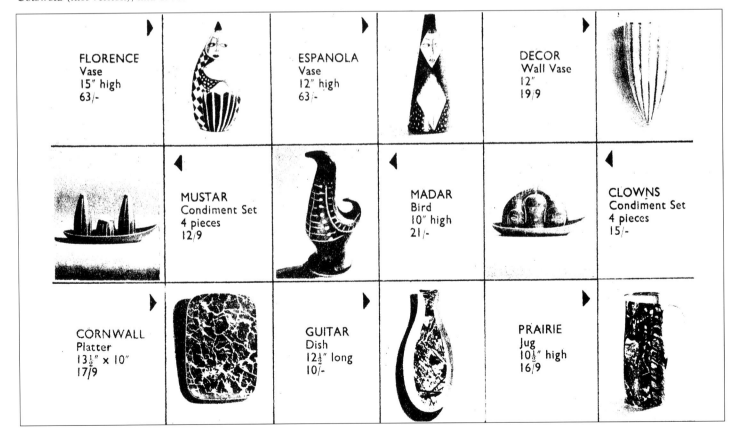

**Tigo Ware** (continued), mid-1950s.

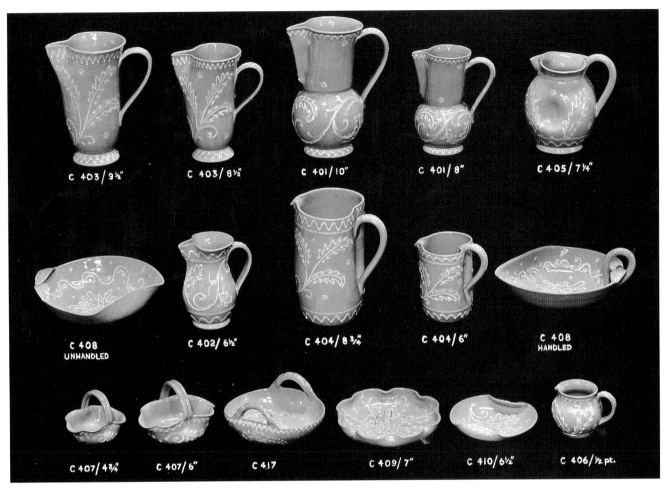

**Celadon**, mid-1950s.

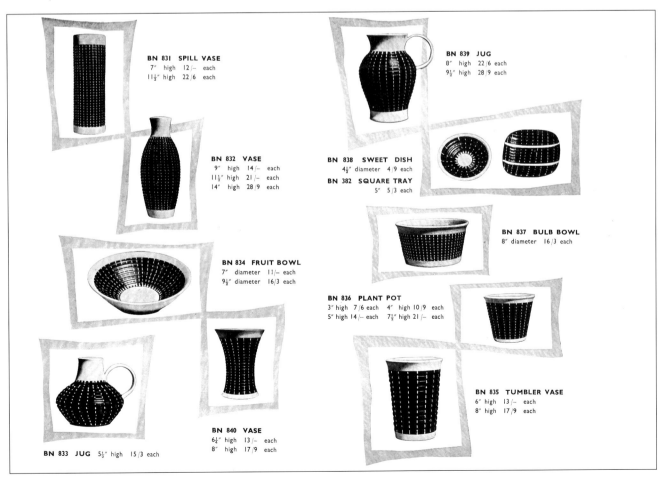

**Burlington**, c.1959.

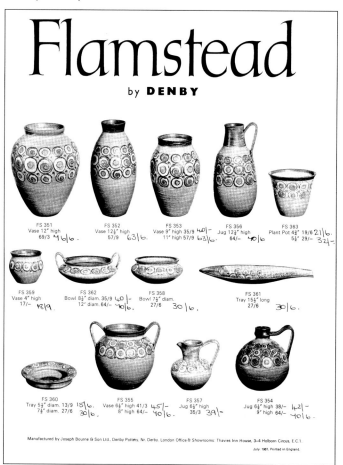

Flamstead, c.1966/7.

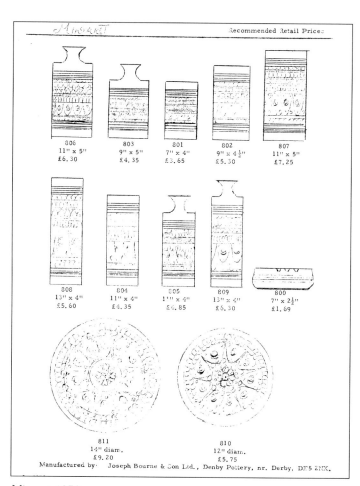

Minaret 1970.

Cascade, c.1978.

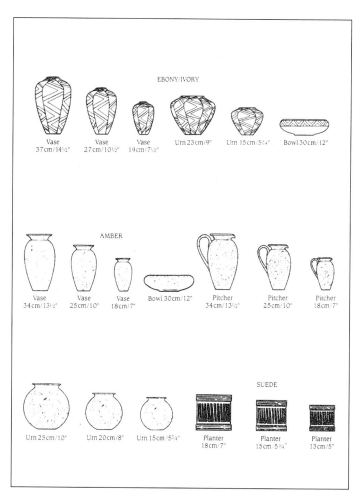

Origins, c.1987.

# DENBY IMPRESSED MARKS AND BACKSTAMPS

The dating of a piece of Denby pottery by its mark or stamp is an inexact science. Many early pots were unmarked. From 1880 to the 1960s some pieces were merely stamped 'MADE IN ENGLAND'. Several backstamps ran concurrently. Some stamps existed for a brief period, others for decades. Minor variations of a particular stamp were prevalent. Special stamps were used for decorative ware or special ranges of table or cook ware. To these, and to 'signed' pieces, would usually be added a general, contemporary 'Denby' or 'MADE IN ENGLAND' backstamp. Some ranges of exported tableware bore a ram's head backstamp encircled by the words 'AUTHENTIC ENGLISH STONEWARE HANDCRAFTED IN ENGLAND' e.g. on Canterbury. Specific retailers often had their own stamp added to ranges produced under contract, e.g. Richards, Mortlock, Comoy and Hill-Ouston. As no written records exist, this list of impressed marks and backstamps has been derived from a variety of sources: the marks on 'dated' pots and pots for which the production period has been confirmed, discussion with Denby experts and general sleuthing through the Denby archives. To date, the trail is incomplete. A single impressed letter on the base of a pot indicated the craftsman, usually the turner or figureman, who had worked on the pot. A coloured dot or dots or hand-painted initial or initials would identify a paintress. The earliest dates listed below are the earliest date or approximate date of which evidence is known to exist.

The authors wish to thank Bruce Edwards for his help in the compilation of this list.

## IMPRESSED MARKS

1. c.1833
Impressed mark on Reform Cordial Flasks.

2. c.1860
Impressed mark on bottles and containers.

3. c.1890
Impressed mark on bottles.

4. c.1890
Impressed mark on bottles and containers.

5. c.1890
Impressed mark on bottles and containers.

6. c.1890-1910
Majolica impressed mark.

7. c.1895
The fleur-de-lys impressed mark of Horace Elliott on sgraffito ware, sometimes impressed Elliott, London.

8. c.1895
The incised monogram of James Wheeler on sgraffito ware.

9 & 10. c.1895
The two most common impressed marks.

11. 1897
Impressed mark with registration number.

12. c.1901-1909
Impressed mark on bottles and containers on which the number is believed to record the year of production.

## BACKSTAMPS
Special stamps or signatures are usually accompanied by a basic 'Denby' or 'Made in England' backstamp.

13. c.1900
A variation of the first 'fired on' stamp.

14. c.1905-1920
'England' was added to the stamp on an informal oval shaped format. There at least three distinct variants, characterised by the depth of the stamp and the size and spacing of the letters.

15. c.1906-1940
British Fireproof Cookware.

16. c.1910
Backstamp on Butterfly Ware.

17. 1915-1930s
The common 'lined' stamp of which there are several variants.

18. c.1924
Standard diamond-shaped logo, of which two sizes are known.

19. 1920s
This stamp first
appeared on its own
in a thick heavy
script.

20. 1930s
Used in conjunction
with either stamp 17
or 18. Other versions
exist with slightly
different script.

21. c.1937
Alice Teichtner
monogram with heavy
scripted Denby stamp.

22. c.1933
Individual stamp for
Epic oven-to-table
ware.

23. 1945-1950s
Oval stamp on
domestic and Gift
Ware.

24. 1945-1950s
Gift Ware stamp. Also
found without the
word Derby in the
circle.

25. c.1948-1958
Glyn Colledge hand-
painted signature in
green on Glyn Ware. A
'Made in England'
stamp was added to this
design.

26. c.1954
Glyn Colledge hand-
painted signature
usually in brown and
occasionally in blue or
green on New Glyn
Ware and, from 1956,
on Cheviot Ware.

27. c.1960
Glyn Colledge
signature stamped on
Glynbourne. Other
versions exist.

28. c.1950-1975
The common scroll
backstamp.

29. c.1954
Individual stamp for
Peasant tableware.

30. c.1956-1977
Individual stamp for
Greenwheat
tableware.

31. c.1962-1977
Individual stamp for
Chevron tableware.

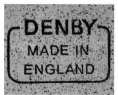

32. c.1975-1985
Standard logo for
tableware and
decorative ware.

33. c.1975-1987
Stamp used on
Renaissance range.

34. 1975-1987
Used predominantly on
imported fine china of
the period. Also used
on some stoneware, eg
Renaissance range with
pattern name shown.

35. 1980-85
Backstamp including
pattern name.

36. 1980-1987
Backstamp including
pattern name.

37. 1980-1987
A specific stamp used
on the Bakewwell
range.

38. 1980s
In general use during
the 1980s.

39. Mid 1980s

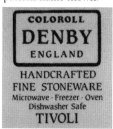

40. 1987-1990
Backstamp including
pattern name.

41. c.1987-1990

42. 1990-1993
Craftsmen workshop
stamp, 1990-1993.

43. c.1991-1995
Classic range ware
(since replaced by
Chefs Ware).

44. 1990s-present day.

45. 1990s-present day.
Used specifically for
hand thrown pottery,
usually on companion
pieces to tableware
ranges.

46. 1990s-present day
Current stamp with
pattern name. The
pattern name was
added in 1993.

47. 1990s-present
day.

48. 1995-present day
Usually associated
with hand thrown
items from the craft
room.

# BIBLIOGRAPHY

Askey, Derek *Stoneware Bottles (1500-1949)*, Bowman Graphics

Bergeson, Victoria *Encyclopaedia of British Art Pottery*, Barrie & Jenkins

Bergeson, Victoria *Price Guide to British Ceramics*, Barrie & Jenkins

Brown, Ronald *History of Derbyshire Potteries*, Northern Ceramics Society

Haslam, Malcolm *The Martin Brothers, Potters*, Richard Dennis Publications

Hildyard, R.J.C. *Browne Muggs*, Victoria and Albert Museum

Hobson, P.L. *A Guide to the Islamic Pottery of the Near East*, British Museum

Jewitt, Llewellyn *The Ceramic Art of Great Britain*, New Orchard Edition

Methodist Church, *The History of the Pottery of the Methodist Church*

Lewis, J.M. *The Ewenny Potteries*, Museum of Welsh Life

Oswald, Adrian, Hildyard, R.J.C., Hughes, R.G., *English Brown Stoneware 1670 - 1900*, Faber and Faber

Wykes-Joyce, Max *Seven Thousand Years of Pottery and Porcelain*, Owen

*The Pottery Gazette*

# INDEX